Top 25 locator map
(enlarged central area map
on inside back cover)

◄

WITHDRAWN

D1099588

TwinPack
Dubai

ROBIN BARTON

Robin Barton is a London-based journalist and editor, writing about travel, sport and the outdoors for several national newspapers and magazines, including *The Independent on Sunday*, *The Observer* and the *Evening Standard*'s *ES* magazine. He has worked on several travel guides, covering destinations as diverse as London, Scotland, Mexico, Costa Rica and Mallorca.

If you have any comments or suggestions for this guide you can contact the editor at *Twinpacks@theAA.com*

AA Publishing
Find out more about AA Publishing and the wide range of travel publications and services the AA provides by visiting our website at *www.theAA.com/travel*

Contents

About this book

TwinPack Dubai is divided into six sections to cover the six most important aspects of your visit to Dubai. It includes:

- The author's view of the emirate and its people
- Suggested drives and excursions
- The Top 25 sights to visit
- The best of the rest – aspects of Dubai that make it special
- Detailed listings of restaurants, hotels, shops and nightlife
- Practical information

In addition, easy-to-read side panels provide fascinating extra facts and snippets, highlights of places to visit and invaluable practical advice.

CROSS-REFERENCES

To help you make the most of your visit, cross-references, indicated by ➤, show you where to find additional information about a place or subject.

MAPS

The fold-out map in the wallet at the back of the book is a large-scale map of Dubai.

The Top 25 locator maps found on the inside front cover (IFC) and inside back cover (IBC) of the book itself are for quick reference. They show the Top 25 sights, described on pages 24–48, which are clearly plotted by number (**1** – **25**, not page number) in alphabetical order.

PRICES

Where appropriate, an indication of the cost of an attraction is given by 💷 Expensive, Moderate or Inexpensive. An indication of the cost of a restaurant is given by $ signs: $$$ denotes higher prices, $$ denotes average prices, while $ denotes lower prices.

DUBAI
life

A Personal View

It is difficult to imagine, but 30 years ago Dubai was a low-lying desert town relying on trade from the Arabian Gulf. There were no indoor ski slopes, none of the hotels had gold fittings or helipads and the largest shopping areas were the traditional, open-air souks. In a few busy decades, Dubai, propelled by an ambitious ruling family and an economy buoyed by oil money, has become a glittering metropolis of skyscrapers, theme parks and shopping malls. The emirate, one of seven that make up the United Arab Emirates (➤ 9), has raced into the 21st century with a plan to attract millions of holidaymakers to this perpetually sunny corner of the Arabian peninsula. Countless dollars have been spent constructing many of the world's most luxurious hotels and entertainment for their thousands of guests.

Today, Dubai's towers reach ever higher from the surrounding sands, its hotels become ever more opulent and its tourist attractions enter the realm of absurdity: on completion, the Dubailand theme park (currently under construction) will be the largest entertainment park in the world by far, while the ethereal Burj Dubai skyscraper – due for completion 2008 – will be the world's tallest building. Dubai's coastline has been augmented

Luxurious Madinat Jumeirah resort is overlooked by the Burj Al Arab

by two palm-shaped islands, each crammed with villas, marinas and hotels, while offshore The World development enables those with a few million dollars in their pocket to buy an island named after a country of the world.

Should you tire of seeing the world within Dubai, it is easy to travel into the neighbouring emirates

Tempting street food on offer in Bur Dubai

LIVING IN DUBAI

Dubai has attracted expatriate residents since the development boom of the early 1980s. In recent years the laws governing foreign ownership of properties have been considerably relaxed. People from outside the UAE can now own freehold property in Dubai and rent out holiday homes, and the income from these holiday homes does not attract income tax. Many prospective property owners in Dubai buy an off-plan villa or apartment in a development, but these projects have a tendency to run over schedule. It is also important to take sound legal and financial advice before buying in Dubai and don't be swayed by unrealistic projections.

of oil-rich Abu Dhabi or Sharjah, or farther afield to Oman and the Indian Ocean coast. In the other emirates you are likely to encounter more Emiratis thazn in Dubai, where the local population is greatly outnumbered by expatriate workers. However, generous Arab hospitality remains a signature of Dubai and the other emirates. And the city has a relatively relaxed attitude to the visitors it welcomes every year. Yes, you will notice social and cultural restrictions but generally it is a forgiving place.

Dubai is one of those places that polarises opinion: if you don't enjoy a sanitised, somewhat artificial environment or the idea of whiling away hours hunting bargains in a shopping mall or chasing a golf ball, Dubai may not be the best place for you. The summers are brutally hot and the natural scenery is limited to sea and sand. However, anyone who appreciates extraordinary architecture, the world's finest hotels and a bewil-

Dubai is as bustling by night as by day

dering choice of recreation will find Dubai meets their expectations. Even the more adventurous traveller can explore the desert in a 4x4 vehicle or try their hand at snowboarding – on snow or sand. As ever in Dubai, the choice is yours.

Dubai in Figures

GEOGRAPHY
- Position: Dubai lies on the Arabian Gulf coast, at the toe of the Arabian peninsula. It is bordered by Oman and Saudi Arabia; on the other side of the Gulf is Iran.
- Area: 3,900sq km.
- The city is divided by Dubai Creek.
- Deira and Bur Dubai, on either side of Dubai Creek, are the city's oldest districts.
- Inland, the desert is being developed, with an area larger than Manhattan being turned into Dubailand.
- Population: 1.6 million, of whom 20 per cent are Emiratis. The remainder are immigrants, mainly from India and Pakistan.

CLIMATE
- Dubai has a desert climate. Rainfall rarely exceeds 120mm (less than 5in) per year. Temperatures range from a low of 15°C (59°F) in winter to a high of 48°C (118°F) in the summer. Humidity is also extemely high in the summer, exceeding 90 per cent.
- Expect sunshine and blue skies year round.
- Dubai's peak season is October to May. December and January, when the climate is at its mildest, are the busiest months.

ECONOMY
- This tiny Gulf state has evolved from a trading post to a versatile and dynamic economy in little over a century. Dubai has never had vast oil reserves; instead the Maktoum family has encouraged trade.
- Tourism is big business. In 2006, Dubai had 416 hotels, up from 293 a decade earlier, and 6.3 million visitors stayed in them. Vast projects, such as Palm Jumeirah island and Dubailand are intended to attract even more visitors.
- Dubai is experiencing record employment growth based on the assumption that more and more people will want to visit Dubai.

Abras (water taxis) on Dubai Creek

People of Dubai

The United Arab Emirates

Dubai is just one of seven emirates that together form the United Arab Emirates. The largest of the emirates – economically and physically – is Abu Dhabi, which takes the lead on military and political matters. The other emirates are Sharjah, Ajman, Umm Al Quwain, Ras Al Khaimah and Fujairah. Dubai is probably the best known of the emirates, thanks to its promotion of tourism. Each emirate, including Dubai, is ruled by a family dynasty. Dubai's ruling party is the Maktoum family; Dubai's president is Sheikh Mohammed bin Rashid Al Maktoum, who has steered the state towards a bright and exciting future.

The Founding of Dubai

The ruling families of the UAE have often been rivals as well as allies. Dubai Creek, the birthplace of modern Dubai, was initially settled after a family dispute drove one part of Abu Dhabi's ruling family out. In the 1950s, Sheikh Rashid bin Saeed Al Maktoum made the shrewd move of dredging the creek, making it possible for larger cargo ships to dock in Dubai when they couldn't fit into Abu Dhabi.

Local Population

Dubai's population was 1.2 million in 2005, comprising just over a quarter of the UAE's total population. However, very few of Dubai's residents are indigenous Emiratis. In fact, Emiratis account for just 20 per cent of the population – they're vastly outnumbered by immigrants from India and Pakistan, who form 60 per cent of the population. Dubai has encouraged immigration since its days as a desert trading outpost, and Britain and Iran are among the other nations that have sizable populations in the city. There are 250,000 foreign construction workers in Dubai alone, while all the population groups are dwarfed by the number of holidaymakers who visit each year.

THE SEVEN EMIRATES

Abu Dhabi – the largest and most influential, and capital of the UAE

Dubai – second-largest and glitziest emirate

Sharjah – the most traditional emirate and guardian of the UAE's cultural heritage

Ajman – famous for its seafaring history and its dhows

Umm Al Quwain – second-smallest emirate; depends on fishing and farming

Ras Al Khaimah – the most scenic emirate; development has also started here

Fujairah – the only emirate on the east coast, popular with Dubaians for its scenery and beaches

Cycling through the streets of Deira by night

A Chronology

1820 Britain signs agreement with tribal leaders along the Gulf Coast. The British Navy protects the coast from pirates in return for a degree of influence in local affairs.

1833 The Al Maktoum branch of the Bani Yas tribal group relocates from farther up the coast to the area surrounding Dubai Creek.

1892 The individual states – including Dubai – sign agreements with Britain. They manage their internal affairs and Britain deals with foreign matters. The states become known as the Trucial States. The Maktoum family adopts a progressive trading policy, abolishing commercial taxes.

1912 Sheikh Saeed bin Maktoum Al Maktoum takes control of Dubai.

1950s Oil is discovered in the Gulf. Abu Dhabi has the largest reserves but Dubai has enough to kick-start its economy.

1952 The seven ruling families of the region, the emirates, form the Trucial Council. This is the first formal, political bond between the city states. Britain remains closely involved.

1958 Sheikh Rashid bin Saeed Al Maktoum becomes Dubai's ruler. Knowing Dubai's oil supplies are limited, his economic strategy is based on attracting more trade and tourism.

1959 Sheikh Rashid orders the construction of Dubai's first airport.

1960 Dubai's creek is dredged at a cost of $850,000. This allows huge cargo ships that can't dock in Abu Dhabi to offload the equipment that Abu Dhabi needs for its oil industry infrastructure.

1971 The seven emirates gain independence from Britain and form the United Arab Emirates, led by Abu Dhabi's Sheikh Zayed bin Sultan Al Nahyan.

1972	Port Rashid, Dubai's deep-water harbour, opens. Business soon floods into the new port, in part due to the tensions between Iraq and Iran at the far end of the Gulf.
1979	Sheikh Rashid becomes president of the UAE. Dubai's first skyscraper, the Dubai World Trade Centre, is opened.
1985	Dubai's new airline, Emirates, is based at Dubai International Airport. Jebel Ali Free Zone is founded, based around Dubai's second deep-water port, Jebel Ali, the world's largest man-made harbour.
1990	Sheikh Rashid dies and is succeeded by his son, Sheikh Maktoum bin Rashid Al Maktoum.
1994	Sheikh Maktoum's dynamic younger brother, Sheikh Mohammed, is appointed Prince of Dubai.
1996	The first Dubai World Cup horse race is run, with the richest prize purse in the world.
1999	The high-tech Burj Al Arab hotel is opened.
2000	The new Sheikh Rashid Terminal opens at Dubai Airport. By 2004 there are 107 airlines serving 160 destinations from the airport.
2001	Work begins on the vast, man-made offshore island, Palm Jumeirah.
2002	Non-nationals are allowed to own property in Dubai freehold.
2005	The largest shopping mall outside America, the Mall of the Emirates, opens, complete with indoor ski slope.
2006	Sheikh Rashid dies and is succeeded by Sheikh Mohammed. Work begins on the Burj Dubai. The UAE holds its first elections – hand-selected voters choose half the members of an advisory government council.

11

Best of Dubai

*Refreshment time
Middle Eastern style*

*All that glitters...
tempting displays in the
Gold Souk in Deira*

If you have only a short time to visit Dubai, or would like to get a complete picture of the emirate, here are the essentials:

- Take a boat trip down the creek, the source of Dubai's wealth. Life on its banks goes on as it has for more than a century, with dhows unloading goods for the souks; the contrast with the modern Dubai of skyscrapers and luxury hotels couldn't be greater.
- Haggle in the souks of Old Dubai (▶ 46). Bargains are few and far between in Dubai these days, but you can still save money on gold jewellery in Deira's Gold Souk.
- Eat at a Lebanese restaurant for a taste of the best Middle Eastern cooking.
- Ride a camel and camp under the stars on a desert safari.
- Take a daytrip to Hatta, a mountain village about an hour's drive from Dubai (▶ 18). You'll need a four-wheel-drive vehicle to drive in the mountains, but there are rock pools and wadis to explore and it is cooler and quieter in the mountains. On the way, you can detour onto Big Red, a vast sand dune where locals and visitors play in off-road vehicles.
- Let the family cool down and get wet at Wild Wadi, a watery theme park in Jumeirah (▶ 47).
- Soak up some of the views from a hotel bar. Look out on Sheikh Zayed Road from Vu's bar in the Jumeirah Emirates Towers Hotel (▶ 82) or cast your eye over The World and the Palm Islands developments from the Skyview Bar in the Burj Al Arab (▶ 25 and 56).
- Shop till you drop at the Mall of the Emirates (▶ 41), then go skiing on Dubai's first, state-of-the-art indoor ski slope (▶ 45).
- Race night at Nad Al Sheba racecourse takes place on Thursdays during the winter season and is a chance to see the Maktoum family's favourite sport – horse racing (▶ 42 and 59).

DUBAI
how to organise
your time

A Walk Around Bur Dubai

Bur Dubai is one of the oldest neighbourhoods in the city and the most rewarding to explore on foot. Its key sights are strung along the creek.

Start from the Sheikh Saeed Al Maktoum House (► 44) at the mouth of the creek.

With a bus and coach parking area to the right, you'll face the block-like Ministry of Finance and Industry. Follow the creek around to the left until you reach the Bur Dubai *abra* station. Turn right then left into the covered alleyway of the Old Souk. Inside the souk you will pass stalls selling clothes, snacks, fabrics, electronics and, at the Golden Arrows stall, novelties such as shark jawbones. Continue until you reach the end of the souk and the Grand Mosque, which has the tallest minaret of any mosque in Dubai, at 70m.

Before you pass the mosque turn right, away from the creek and uphill.

Textile stalls in Bur Dubai's souk

The Dubai Museum (► 32) in the Al Fahidi Fort is ahead. The entrance is on the far side, past a ship used for pearl diving called a *sambuk*.

After exiting the museum, turn left along Al Fahidi Street, crossing a small intersection to join a strip of neon-lit shops.

At the end of Al Fahidi Street, before the roundabout, you'll arrive at the Majlis Gallery (► 79–80). You can stop for refreshments at the Basta Art Café (► 60) next door.

Turn left to head back to the creek.

Back at the creek you have two options. If you're staying in Deira, turn left along the waterfront and pick up an *abra* from the official station and cross the creek for a trip to the Spice Souk (► 46) for less than 1Dh. Or turn right and hire a private *abra* from the owners on the steps. It will cost 50–70Dh to go up to Creekside Park (► 28).

A Drive to Al Ain

The highest mountain in the United Arab Emirates is Jebel Hafeet, and you can drive all the way to the top and look out over Al Ain.

Al Ain is signposted from Sheikh Zayed Road's Interchange 1. If you're based in Deira, the easiest route is down Garhoud Road, past the airport then right, around the ring road (Route 611), aiming for Academic City, until you see signs for Al Ain and Hatta. Get on the three-lane highway, Route 66, and continue all the way to Al Ain.

Al Ain is known locally as much for its roundabouts as for its gardens; 'Tourists Follow Brown Signs' is the sound advice offered.

Go straight over the first roundabout. At the second roundabout, take the third left for Al Ain's National Archaeological Park (daily 4–11, holidays 10–11, 1Dh).

At the park you'll find exhibits recovered from some of the 5,000-year-old tombs at Hili.

From here, go straight over the next two roundabouts and left at the third. Follow signs for the town centre straight over the next seven roundabouts. Pick up brown signs for Jebel Hafeet and, in green, Mubazzarah. Bear left for Jebel Hafeet, which you will see rising in front of you. Head left again at the roundabout with the mountain sheep sculpture, following signs for Jebel Hafeet and Mubazzarah.

The resort of Mubazzarah has hot springs that are open to visitors. After the Mubazzarah turning, the road gets very twisty and the speed limit is reduced to 30kph for the 13km drive up to the top of Jebel Hafeet. Here you can relax over a snack at the Accor Hotel or watch the sunset and stay the night.

INFORMATION

Distance 100km
Time Half a day
Start/end point Sheikh Zayed Road, Interchange 1 ➕ IFC 2B
Lunch Eden Rock Terrace Restaurant ($$)
✉ Mercure Grand Jebel Hafeet, Al Ain
☎ 03 783 8888

View from Jebel Hafeet

A Drive into Fujairah

The only emirate on the Indian Ocean, Fujairah is blessed with beaches, mountains and lots of winding roads to speed you from one to the other.

INFORMATION

Distance 320km round trip
Time 1 or 2 days, staying overnight at a beach resort (Hilton or Le Meridien in Fujairah)
Start/end point Clock tower roundabout on Al Maktoum Road
➕ IBC 3D
Lunch Sailors Restaurant
✉ Hilton Fujairah Resort
☎ 971 222 2411

From the clock tower roundabout in Deira follow Route 74, signposted Al Sharjah, straight through central Sharjah. Then follow signs for Sharjah airport. Go over the first roundabout you come to, and take the second exit at the next roundabout, all the while following signs for the airport.

You're now on the Al Dhaid road, also known as Route 88, but not signposted as such yet. On the right is Sharjah University, with majestic fountains in the gardens. Then comes Sharjah Discovery Centre, a science theme park for children. Keep in the left lane as you pass the green gardens of Sharjah National Park on the right. Continuing along Route 88, you will pass the Sharjah Arab Culture Monument to your right at Interchange 8. Also off Interchange 8 is the Sharjah Natural History Museum and Desert Park, on the opposite side of the motorway.

The Wildlife Centre has more than 100 species, from vipers to oryx. A nocturnal house allows visitors to observe species such as the mongoose, honey badger and jackal.

Return to Route 88 and continue to Al Dhaid (now signposted). On entering Al Dhaid, turn left at the first roundabout, driving down the shop-lined main street. Turn right at the next roundabout and go straight over the next, staying on Route 88 and following signs for Masafi. Stay on this wide, well-made road until it reaches Fujairah, after winding through the barren hills.

To go straight to the seafront, follow signs for the corniche, which will take you straight ahead at most of the roundabouts. The Hilton resort lies at the north end of the corniche and is a good place for refreshments. At weekends the seafront from the Hilton south to Kalba is crowded with beachgoers enjoying the gardens and sandy beach. There are plenty of parking spaces.

Fujairah is the newest emirate, since it was part of Sharjah until 1952. To visit the Fujairah Museum, turn left after you enter Fujairah and follow signposts.

From Fujairah it is 55km north to Dibba, following Route 99. Stick to Corniche Street (seafront) through the town of Khor Fakkan, straight over the roundabouts and past the petrol station styled like a castle. After Khor Fakkan, look for Al Bidiyah mosque on the left, which dates from 1446.

You can stop and look around the exterior of the mosque outside prayer times. Bidiyah village itself dates from around 3000 BC and is one of the oldest settlements on the Indian Ocean coast.

At the next turning, bear right on Route 87 for the pretty town of Dibba. There's an incongruous high-rise resort (Le Meridien's Al Aqah Beach Resort) before you enter the town.

From Dibba you can charter a boat to take you to Snoopy Island (the profile of the island looks like the cartoon character in repose), where there is excellent diving and snorkelling.

Dibba was the site of many battles between Islamic forces from Saudi Arabia and Arab tribesmen in the 6th and 7th centuries; the Islamists won, leaving huge cemeteries at Dibba.

Fujairah's roads are managed by a series of roundabouts, often interestingly ornamented

After you exit Dibba, turn left onto Route 18 and after 10km take the right exit for Sharjah. You're now back on Route 88 so retrace your steps through Al Dhaid and Sharjah. On passing Sharjah airport and the university, turn left at the roundabout at the end of the Route 88 and go ahead at the next roundabout for Dubai. Do not enter Sharjah, since the roads are poorly signposted and you will get lost; if you miss the turning, turn around and try again.

A Drive to Hatta

INFORMATION

Distance 120km
Time 1 day, or stay overnight
at the Hatta Fort hotel
Start end/point Sheikh Zayed
Road, Interchange 1
⊞ IFC 2B
Lunch Hatta Fort Hotel ($$)
☎ 971 852 3211

Hatta is a small mountain town with two important attractions – a fine hotel and a series of rock pools that are a 45-minute off-road drive into the mountains. The one-hour drive to Hatta is easy enough, but you'll need detailed directions to the pools; you can pick these up from the Hatta Fort Hotel. You need the blue route pack.

Take Route 44 out of Dubai, signposted from Interchange 1 on Sheikh Zayed Road. This road will take you all the way to Hatta.

About halfway to Hatta, a number of quad and motorbike tour operators have set up shop. In the distance, the rust-coloured Big Red is the largest and most famous dune in Dubai and provides an irresistible challenge to off-road drivers.

As you enter Hatta you'll encounter a roundabout: Hatta Fort Hotel (► 36) is to the left, and Hatta and its attractions are to the right. If you carry straight on you'll enter Oman after 10km. Ignore signs for Hill Park and continue uphill through the town until you see the signs for Hatta Heritage Village to the left. The road twists and turns until it reaches the village, which was opened in 2001 and aims to show what life was like in the mountains.

Desert driving is a whole new challenge: don't venture off road unless you know what you're doing

On leaving the village stay on the same road and continue away from Hatta. At the next junction (a roundabout in front of a mosque), bear left. After 1km take the second right, down what looks like a residential road with speed bumps. Follow this road for 7km through Qiman village and on the other side take the track to the right.

This is the route to Hatta's rock pools, a 10km off-road drive along dirt tracks and wadis (dried-up waterways) to a parking area. If you started early and want to make a day of it, you can continue past the rock pools and drive along a series of wadis to make a circuit back to the Hatta Fort Hotel. It's a 121km route and should take six hours; follow the detailed directions of the hotel's blue route map.

Jumeirah's Beaches

Golden sand, clear blue sea and reliable, even roasting, sunshine: Dubai's beaches appeal to many visitors.

All Dubai's beaches, except the public beach at Al Mamzar Beach Park, are on the Jumeirah side of the Creek. The coast stretches from the built-up suburbs behind Jumeirah public beach near Port Rashid all the way to Jebel Ali port, a distance of some 40km. The shore is a mix of free public beaches, public beach parks where a nominal entry is charged and private beaches managed by hotels. Hotel beaches are often cleaned and may have facilities such as changing area, sun loungers, refreshments and water sports. If you are staying at a city-centre hotel that has a sister hotel with a beach you may be allowed to use it free of charge; this applies to the Sheraton, Le Meridien, Jumeirah and Hilton hotels among others. Dubai's shore has no bays so breakwaters are used to partition the beach.

In general, water quality is good, but note that there is an undertow, so weak swimmers should stick to the hotel swimming pool. Some beaches may provide a lifeguard and may forbid swimming when there is no lifeguard on duty.

Dubai's authorities are placing increasing restrictions on water sports such as jet skiing and kitesurfing on the public beaches. Jebel Ali beach is Dubai's most unspoiled beach but the plan to build the Jebel Ali Palm Island at the nearside may change this. Currently this beach is popular with kitesurfers and those who want to laze among real sand dunes.

BEST PRIVATE BEACHES

Le Meridien Mina Seyahi Beach Resort and Marina ➤ 52

Sheraton Jumeirah Beach Resort and Towers ➤ 53

One&Only Royal Mirage Hotel ➤ 73

Habtoor Grand Resort and Spa ➤ 72

The Ritz-Carlton ➤ 53

Jumeirah Beach Hotel ➤ 71

Oasis Beach Hotel ➤ 53

Hilton Dubai Jumeirah
🏷 100Dh (Sat–Thu), 130Dh (Fri); facilities include kids club and beach activities ☎ 399 1111

Dubai's best beaches are along the Jumeirah seafront

19

Finding Peace & Quiet

Dubai is a city in perpetual motion – except during rush hour when traffic comes to a halt – and the ever-expanding concrete environment can become stressful. But, remarkably, there are still places in the city where you can relax in serene surroundings. In Dubai, however, every-thing, peace and quiet included, has a price, and solitude comes at a premium.

HOTEL RETREATS

The most obvious places to find peace and quiet are in the spas of the luxury hotels – the individual treatment rooms in the most expensive spas often have such soothing features as a personal waterfall cascading over pebbles. Many of the major hotels also have their own tropical gardens where you can watch birds and insects living in blissful ignorance of the sprawling cityscape around them: the Ritz-Carlton and the Sheraton Jumeirah Beach Resort in West Jumeirah have particularly attractive gardens, while the Emirates Towers Hotel has a zen garden at its base. The next best position is beside the private swimming pools, although beware cavorting children. Some pools will be designated adults-only and rooftop pools, such as that at the Shangri-La hotel, also boast great views.

SPORT

Sports also offer the opportunity to get away from it all: you can charter a motorboat or yacht from marinas on the Creek and escape to the sea. Or book a round of golf.

BELOW THE WAVES

Perhaps the most peaceful place to be in the Emirates is underwater. Scuba diving is an increasingly popular activity, with dive outfits offering PADI-accredited courses and a variety of trips to experienced divers. There are several operators in Dubai who can take you wreck diving in the Arabian Gulf; find an operator at www.padi.com. On the east coast, from Fujairah, you can explore coral reefs in the Indian Ocean with dive operators such as Scuba 2000 (www.scuba-2000.com).

Zabeel Park provides some welcome greenery in busy downtown

PARKS

Dubai's velvety-green golf courses are not the only green oases in the city. Vast desalination plants work 24 hours a day turning sea water into fresh water, which is used to irrigate the city's parks as well as the golf courses. Two parks, Zabeel (► 48) and Creekside (► 28), are appealing refuges from the hurly-burly of downtown Dubai, although Creekside Park in particular becomes very crowded during the weekends. The flowerbeds in Creekside Park are planted with indigenous desert-dwelling plants (you can find out more about local flora and fauna in the Dubai Museum, ► 32), and these cleverly designed gardens are designed to be explored away from the park's main thoroughfares. Unsurprisingly, the city's beach parks, Al Mamzar in Deira and Al Safa in Jumeirah, are also extremely popular during the weekends.

The cable cars over Creekside Park are a popular attraction

OUTSIDE DUBAI

For naturally occurring gardens you should travel into Abu Dhabi. The neighbouring emirate's second city, Al Ain (► 15), is known as the Garden City, thanks to a series of city-centre oases. Water from these oases feeds parks and gardens that are surprisingly lush. You can get a good impression of the city's greenery from the top of Jebel Hafeet mountain. Another place where underground water fills wadis is Hatta – but the last thing you should expect at the famous rock pools is peace and quiet.

THE DESERT

But there's one place where peace and quiet, if not quite guaranteed, is certainly more likely, and that is outside Dubai on a 4x4 trip through the desert. You can take an organised safari or venture off road in a small group of vehicles (► 57, panel for tips on driving safely in the desert).

What's On

JANUARY

Dubai Shopping Festival (can run into Feb): shops discount stock by up to 80 per cent. Associated events include outdoor music shows and children's activities.

FEBRUARY

Dubai Desert Golf Competition: usually takes place at the Emirates Golf Club. It has been part of Europe's PGA Tour since 1989.
Dubai Tennis Open: held at the Aviation Club's courts on Garhoud Road. Competitors include top seeds, all serving for the $1 million prize money.
Dubai International Jazz Festival: A diverse selection of performers is booked for the three-night festival.

MARCH

Dubai International Boat Show: Your chance to see the world's most expensive yachts and cruisers in close-up at the Dubai International Marine Club in Mina Seyahi.
Dubai World Cup: The world's richest horse race, at the Nad Al Sheba racecourse. The World Cup race itself, always held on a Saturday, is the climax of the Dubai Racing Carnival.

JUNE

Dubai Summer Surprises: A reprise of the January shopping festival.
Dubai Traditional Dhow Races: The six-race series concludes in June.

SEPTEMBER

Ramadan: Shops change their opening times and restaurants may not serve alcohol during the month-long fast. The dates vary every year.

OCTOBER

Eid Al Fitr: The three-day festival at the end of Ramadan is the liveliest holiday for Muslims and there are feasts and parties all over the city.

NOVEMBER

UAE Desert Challenge: The Emirates' premier off-road driving race. The event starts near Abu Dhabi and ends four days later near Dubai.

DECEMBER

Dubai International Film Festival: Inaugurated in 2004, the festival is gaining in popularity every year.
Seven-a-side rugby tournament: Dubai's expats come out to play.

DUBAI'S
top 25 sights

The sights are shown on the maps on the inside front cover and inside back cover, numbered **1**–**25** alphabetically

Bastakiya

INFORMATION

➕ IBC 2B
✉ Sheikh Mohammed
Centre for Cultural
Understanding, Al Seef
roundabout
☎ 353 6666;
www.cultures.ae
🍴 Cafés and restaurants
🔁 Dubai Museum (➤ 32)

Bastakiya was once an affluent neighbourhood of traders. Today the houses are art galleries, cultural centres and restaurants.

Bastakiya is a collection of about 50 restored buildings on the shore of the creek, dating back to the 1900s when Iranian traders settled here. It is one of the oldest heritage sites in Dubai and you can pass through it if you take a creekside stroll or visit some of the attractions nearby, such as the Dubai Museum. The best way to experience the area is to explore it on a winter evening when the smell of Arabic food wafts from restaurants and dhows ply the creek as they have done for hundreds of years.

All the buildings in Bastakiya are made of coral walls covered with a sand plaster and feature an ancient form of air-conditioning using windtowers. Now these buildings are art galleries, museums, shops and restaurants – all subtly integrated into the historic surroundings. The Sheikh Mohammed Centre for Cultural Understanding in Bastakiya explains Emirati life in detail and can organise a guide if required.

Bastakiya is an early example of the shrewd forward thinking of Dubai's rulers: they granted Iranian traders tax concessions and easy immigration in much the same way as today's government encourages immigration. The whole

Elegant striped pillars on a restored building, Bastakiya

neighbourhood is largely car-free, which offers some respite from Bur Dubai's bustle. This is also a good point from which to take boats to explore other areas of the creek.

Burj Al Arab

This futuristic marvel sums up Dubai's forward-looking, upwardly mobile attitude. Admire the view from the Skyview Bar over a cocktail.

It is fitting that Dubai's iconic building isn't a government edifice, a historic landmark or a place of religious worship; rather, it's a hotel. Architect Thomas Wills Wright and builders WS Atkins were briefed to create something that would signal Dubai's ambitions to the world, but there are also references to Dubai's seafaring past in the sail-like façade made of a Teflon-coated, woven glass-fibre material. During the day it's a retina-burning white, but at night it becomes the back-drop to a technicolour lightshow visible from the hotels along Jumeirah beach.

The Burj Al Arab stands on its own man-made island 280m offshore; getting past the security guards at the bridge's gatehouse requires a reservation at one of the hotel's restaurants or bars. It's worth the effort though, not only for the views of The World development, but also to see the interior decoration. Credited to Kuan Chew of KCA International, the red, yellow and blue swirly carpets and gold and silver plating are enough to make you seasick. And if it looks like gold it probably is: 1,600sq m of 24-carat gold leaf were used.

The hotel's other vital statistics are equally jaw-dropping: there are 1,500 members of staff for 202 suites, each of which has its own butler. A fleet of 10 white Rolls-Royces is at the disposal of guests, while a helicopter shuttle service from the airport costs 9,000Dh. Perhaps the highlight of a visit to the Burj Al Arab is the high-speed exterior lift, which whisks passengers to the top floor at an ear-popping 6m per second.

INFORMATION

➕ IFC 1B
✉ Beach Road, Jumeirah
☎ 301 7777;
www.burj-al-arab.com
🔁 Madinat Jumeirah
(► 39), Wild Wadi
(► 47)

The unmistakable Burj Al Arab looms up before you as you head down Beach Road

Burj Dubai

INFORMATION

➕ IFC 2B

✉ Near Interchange 1,
Sheikh Zayed Road

☎ www.burjdubai.com

🍴 On-site restaurants, cafés,
bars

🔄 Falcon and Heritage
Sports Centre (▶ 50),
Godolphin Gallery
(▶ 35), Nad Al Sheba
(▶ 42)

Destined to be one of the wonders of the world, the ethereal Burj Dubai is almost 1km high, with amazing views of the emirates from the top.

At the time of writing, Burj Dubai was growing floor by floor, day by day. When it is complete it will be the tallest manmade structure in the world, although no one is quite sure yet when the builders will stop: somewhere between 700m and 900m is the best guess. One thing is certain: Burj Dubai will be the most astounding building in Dubai and perhaps the world.

Architect Adrian Smith of Skidmore, Owings and Merrill found inspiration for the Y-shaped base of the tower in a desert flower's petals. The triple-lobed shape helps resist the region's strong winds, while an outer layer of reflective glazing and steel and aluminium panels will withstand the ferocious heat of the Dubai summer. Some details are known about what will be inside the tower. A Giorgio Armani hotel will occupy several of the lower floors. Above the hotel will be private apartments, many of which sold within eight hours of going on sale. An observation deck will be located on the 124th floor. Outside, there will be shopping, entertainment and residential developments to rival the Dubai Marina.

Interestingly, Burj Dubai will entitle the Middle East to claim ownership of the world's tallest structure for the first time since the 1300s, when Britain's Lincoln Cathedral took the honour from Egypt's Great Pyramid, which had held the title for the preceding 38 centuries.

How the finished tower will look

BurJuman Centre

Highly stylish, central and compact, the BurJuman Centre leads the way for shoppers in Bur Dubai, particularly for women's fashion.

Entering BurJuman is a little like entering an Escher drawing – the farther you venture in, the bigger it gets and the more angular the design becomes. Successive expansions mean that BurJuman currently has 300 outlets. The emphasis at this central mall is on high fashion. Out of the 95 shops selling womenswear, the most notable is a branch of Saks 5th Avenue. The store takes up two levels, the lower level housing the cosmetics and perfume counters, the men's area and the café. The second level of Saks is where you'll find the designer labels and jewellery.

BurJuman's shops are a good mix of the exclusive names – Dior, Lacroix, Dolce & Gabbana, Hermes, Tiffany & Co. – with more affordable retailers such as Gap and Zara. Shoppers hunting for a more laid-back look can try Diesel, Levi's or Quiksilver. When you're shopped out, there are 15 fast-food outlets, 17 cafés (including Starbucks and Dome) and nine restaurants to choose from. Take the escalator up to the top floor, where several cafés and restaurants surround a rooftop garden, which benefits from natural light coming through the sculpted glass roof. For families with young children there's a mother-and-baby room and the Fun City entertainment area.

A tourist information booth on level one of the North Village (☎ 352 0003) can help you plan the rest of your day.

INFORMATION

- ✚ IBC 1B
- ✉ Trade Centre Road
- ☎ 352 0222; www.burjuman.com
- 🕐 Sat–Thu 10–10, Fri 2–10, some stores later on Fri
- 🍴 Many cafés, including Dome and Starbucks
- ♿ Good
- ❓ Valet parking for a nominal charge

Western designer brands are keen to get in on the Dubai action

Creekside Park

INFORMATION

- IBC 2D
- Riyadh Road
- 971 336 7633
- Fri–Tue 8am–11pm, Wed–Thu 8am–11.30pm
- Snacks from stalls in the park
- Inexpensive
- Good
- Children's City (➤ 50), Wonderland (➤ 50)
- Bicycle hire from Gate 2 for additional fee

Respite from Dubai's hectic traffic is granted in this superb park on the shores of the creek. Families will find it especially entertaining.

Creekside, with something for everyone, is the best park in Dubai. Active types can explore the 2.5km of shoreline on rented bicycles and gardeners can enjoy the themed gardens containing 280 plant species. Sightseers will marvel at the sensational views and families will love the open space and activities. At 222ha, Creekside is a very large park; you should allocate at least half a day to do it justice. The best idea is to wander from one end to the other, following the sign-posted paths that pique your interest. Pagodas and landscaped gardens are sequestered among the park's slopes; the desert garden features indigenous desert-dwelling plants, while the date palmgrove is interspersed with traditional Arabic watchtowers. On weekends, families come to cook barbecues and laze about in the sun (remember swimwear is only acceptable on the beach). Some bring fishing tackle to try their luck from the piers, while others take the mini-train around the park's perimeter.

Chilling out on the green lawns of Creekside Park

But the main attraction of Creekside Park is its cable-car system, which runs along a stretch of shoreline 30m above the ground. The cars provide fantastic views of the Dubai Creek Golf Club (➤ 78), an elegant building on the opposite side of the creek intended to resemble the sails of a dhow. There are several gates accessing the park, each with a car park.

Dubai Creek

The story of the creek echoes Dubai's development from a desert trading post to the modern city it is today. Both aspects of Dubai still exist here.

In the 19th century the Maktoum family relocated from Abu Dhabi to Dubai – a small village beside an inlet to the north of the capital. Dubai slowly prospered and development stretched inland along both sides of the creek. The pearl-fishing industry, based in the creek, brought money to the port and Dubai became known as a place that welcomed non-Arab immigrants. But it wasn't until the creek was dredged in 1960 and Abu Dhabi struck oil, making Dubai's deep-water port essential for importing drilling equipment, that Dubai took off.

You don't have to go far to see what life on the creek was like decades ago. Between the Maktoum Bridge and the Sheraton Dubai Creek Hotel is where dhows moor for the night, undergo repairs and refuel for the next leg of their voyage. And from the Radisson SAS hotel down to the mouth of the inlet, Deira's creekside is lined with boats unloading everything from vegetables to TVs – despite the property deals being made elsewhere, this is very much a working port.

An *abra* crossing is an essential Dubai experience. These narrow boats motor back and forth across the creek from station to station and from them you can see both the modern highrise glass towers and the windtowers and minarets of old Dubai. It is the quickest and most enjoyable way to cross the creek. As you pass under Maktoum Bridge and the creek widens, the Dubai Creek Golf and Yacht Club has a new marina with space for 300 yachts. Then the creek curves round to the right and broadens out into the Ras Al Khor lagoon, haven of flamingos and other migratory birds.

INFORMATION

➕ IBC 3B
🍴 Numerous cafés

The best way to cross the creek is by abra

Dubailand

INFORMATION

➕ IFC 3C

✉ Reached via Dubai–Al Ain road or several other access points from Sheikh Zayed Road

☎ www.dubailand.ae

🍴 Many restaurants when completed

Dubailand is Dubai's most ambitious project. With most of the buildings still to emerge, it is hard to imagine what the huge complex will look like.

Six vast, themed worlds comprise Dubailand, the personal project of Sheikh Mohammed. At the time of writing they were Attractions and Experiences World, Retail and Entertainment World, Leisure and Vacation World, Eco-Tourism World, Sports and Outdoor World and Downtown. The content of each world has not been finalized, but some highlights are known. Attractions and Experiences World will include a water park, another indoor ski resort, Kids' City and Arabian theme parks. Construction has already begun on Global Village, a retail area representing countries and cultures from around the world.

Dubailand's Global Village

Eco-Tourism World will be home to Bio World, the Science and History Museum, Desert Camps and Dinosaur World, developed with assistance from London's Natural History Museum. Downtown will have the world's largest observation wheel and the world's largest shopping mall.

Sports and Outdoor World, the vanguard of Dubai's drive to become the sporting capital of the world, will boast an equestrian and polo club, Dubai Golf City, Sports City and the Autodrome, which opened in 2005. Sports City will have a Manchester United Soccer Academy and 65,000-seat stadium.

Seven of these projects should open in 2008, with completion of the entire Dubailand due a decade later. By this time, developers are planning for annual visitor numbers of 15 million, with a further 300,000 people employed at Dubailand's attractions or in its 55 hotels. An estimate for the final, total cost of Dubailand is 65 billion Dh ($18 billion).

Dubai Marina

Vast, ocean-going motorboats are moored in this expanding marina, surrounded by a forest of towers. It is now a popular place for socialising.

The centrepiece of a second axis to the city, Dubai Marina combines leisure and residential facilities on the waterway that runs inland around the luxury hotels of Al Sufouh. It's a man-made harbour, and the developers have placed plenty of vantage points all around the perimeter so you can see what is going on.

The best way to appreciate the marina is to stroll along the waterfront on a winter evening, watching the diners on the restaurant terraces and the dazzling lights of the skyscrapers. Property prices are high here, with two-bedroom apartments starting at 1 million Dh; luxury four- or five-bed pads can cost many times as much.

The marina is a super spot for water sports fans. The Dubai International Marine Club, headquartered next to Le Meridien Mina Seyahi Hotel, organises races for almost every category of sea-going craft, including the Gulf's premier powerboat racing series, dhow racing, and races for jet-skis, keelboats and dinghies. There are car parks at the entrance of the marina, just off the busy Interchange 5 of Sheikh Zayed Road, where a taxi rank awaits. The boardwalk to the left and the right of the entrance is where many of the mostly unlicensed restaurants are located. On weekends, families come here and while the children play in the ornamental fountains, dad smokes a shisha in a café. The marina has curiosity value alone – how often do you see a forest of almost 100 skyscrapers being built? – but remember that it is surrounded by a construction site. Residents have to clean their cars of dust once a day.

INFORMATION

- ➕ IFC 1C
- ✉ Dubai International Marine Club
- ☎ 399 5777; www.dimc-nae.com
- 🍴 Some restaurants around perimeter of marina
- ♿ Some ramps, otherwise good

Luxury boats berthed ready for action

Dubai Museum

INFORMATION

➕ IBC 2A
✉ Al Fahidi Street
☎ 353 1862
🕐 Sat–Thu 8.30–8.30, Fri
   2.30–8.30; daily
   9–midnight during
   Ramadan
👤 Inexpensive
♿ Poor
🔁 Bastakiya (➤ 24)

Find out how the city has changed in Dubai Museum's superb underground extension. If you go to only one museum in Dubai, make it this one.

Housed in the 18th-century Al Fahidi Fort, the museum is made up of a series of galleries describing life around Dubai over the 5,000-year history of the settlement, from its trading and seafaring origins, through the pearl-diving period, conflict, the oil boom and finally the current construction fever. The fort was built to protect the traders and seafarers living at the mouth of Dubai's creek from invasion.

A threadbare stuffed flamingo welcomes visitors to the new galleries under the courtyard, which have sections on archaeology, traditional housing, the souk in 1950, the desert, the mosque, marine life and astronomy. Models show the lives of merchants, boat-builders, potters and jewellers. The architecture room shows how windtowers used to cool houses.

An exhibition on the Bedouin people explains why water was a constant obsession – without it they couldn't water their sheep or camels. Another interesting section throws light on desert ecology and how plants and animals survive average temperatures of 40°C in summer and just 120mm of rain annually. But the most fascinating tableau is that of the pearl diver. Divers worked in the region for a thousand years and by the turn of the 20th century there were about 300 pearl-diving dhows. The men would sail to the pearl beds (Al Hiraat) and make incredibly deep dives with only a turtleshell noseclip, a rope basket, a stone weighing 5kg to pull them down and a rope looped around their foreheads to guide them back up. The final gallery has displays of pre-Christian objects found near Dubai: bronze daggers, arrowheads, shell buttons and more.

Fortress on the outside, museum on the inside

Dubai World Trade Centre

See where Dubai's transformation from desert trading outpost to home of world-class skyscrapers really kicked off – at the city's first tower.

INFORMATION

➕ IFC 2B
✉ Trade Centre Roundabout
☎ 332 1000
♿ Disabled access
↔ Emirates Towers (➤ 34), Zabeel Park (➤ 48)

The Dubai World Trade Centre has a single, but significant, claim to fame. This honeycombed structure, 149m tall, was Dubai's first skyscraper when it was completed in 1979. Since then, ever more elaborate skyscrapers have marched down Sheikh Zayed Road. It might look dated, but the World Trade Centre tower was the precursor to modern Dubai. It still performs a valuable function, housing an impressive array of international businesses, a reasonably priced hotel and several consulates in its 39 storeys – and is one of the most popular venues for weddings in the UAE. To see how far Dubai has come in 25 years, pull out a 100Dh note and hold the image of the Dubai World Trade Centre on it up against the newest skyscraper in Dubai's skyline: Burj Dubai (➤ 26).

Dubai has one great advantage over other world cities when it comes to constructing new buildings: an abundance of empty land. The World Trade Centre was built out of the desert, and today's developers have a blank canvas stretching around them. Architects are encouraged by Dubai's leader, Sheikh Mohammed, to create increasingly amazing landmarks for his city. Apart from the Burj Dubai, the list includes the Dubai Creek Golf and Yacht Club, the Emirates Towers on Sheikh Zayed Road and the Burj Al Arab hotel. Dubai is not shy about advertising its architectural ambitions – 'The Future is Now' and 'History Rising' are among the slogans plastered on billboards around building sites. But it's wise to remember that all this began with one building in the 1970s, the Dubai World Trade Centre.

Still imposing, the Dubai World Trade Centre soars above the palm trees

33

Emirates Towers

INFORMATION

➕ IFC 2B

✉ Sheikh Zayed Road

☎ 330 0000

🍴 Restaurants and bars in
the Jumeirah Emirates
Towers hotel and cafés in
the Boulevard mall

🔁 Dubai World Trade Centre
(➤ 33)

These futuristic twin towers were the first of Dubai's skyscrapers to test the boundaries of what could be created.

The two Emirates Towers are the stars of Dubai's architectural hall of fame. Standing at the gateway of Sheikh Zayed Road, they draw the eye with a remarkable charisma and a science-fiction other-worldliness. The contrast with the Dubai World Trade Centre couldn't be greater: the city's first skyscraper retains a certain 1970s charm, but the Emirates Towers are currently Dubai's most compelling creation. Their piercing apexes symbolize Dubai's drive to succeed.

Designed by the Norr Group, the taller of the towers was completed in November 1999 at an

There are many sophisticated refreshment options in the Emirates Towers

official height of 354.6m. Its shorter partner (at 305m and 56 storeys) was completed on 15 April 2000. Dedicated to the Jumeirah Emirates Towers hotel, it is the second tallest hotel-only structure in the world (➤ 25 for the tallest, Burj Al Arab). The two towers are connected by a 836sq m underground shopping mall, The Boulevard. A visit to Vu's bar (➤ 81) on the 51st floor is essential; the view down a shimmering Sheikh Zayed Road at night makes the prices almost palatable. Alternatively, the Zen garden at the foot of the Emirates Towers is the perfect place to meditate on Dubai, the home of the modern skyscraper.

If seeing the view from the top isn't enough, there's a thoroughly masochistic way of seeing the Emirates Towers: a vertical marathon. Competitors – it's open to anyone – have to run up the 1,334 steps linking the 52 floors of the Jumeirah Emirates Towers hotel, a distance of 265 vertical metres.

Godolphin Gallery

The Godolphin stable's pantheon of world-class horses is second to none, and this gallery conveys some of the excitement of horse racing.

INFORMATION

⊞ IFC 2C
✉ Nad Al Sheba racecourse
(5km south of central
Dubai)
☎ 336 3031;
www.godolphin.com
www.dubairacing.com
◷ Mon–Sun 9–5, on race
nights 9–8
↔ Burj Dubai (➤ 26),
Falcon and Heritage
Sports Centre (➤ 50),
Nad Al Sheba (➤ 42)

The love the Maktoums have for horses and horse racing can't be overstated and the Nad Al Sheba racecourse and neighbouring Godolphin Gallery testify to this obsession. Race Night at Nad Al Sheba should be an essential part of any winter-time visit to Dubai, while all Dubai society turns up for the World Cup races in March.

Even those uninterested in horse racing may enjoy the Godolphin Gallery, a cleverly conceived celebration of horses, racing and winning, opened on Dubai World Cup Day in 1999. There's a trophy gallery, cinema, touch-screen presentations and detailed histories of the Maktoum's most successful horses.

The exhibition space is organised chronologically into smaller galleries, starting from the left of the entrance. In the centre, a cinema plays a rather poetically produced film about the training of the Sheikh's horses in both Dubai and England, where Godolphin keeps stables

The all-wood interior of the Godolphin Gallery

near Newmarket. Special horses have their own showcases in the galleries, with pride of place going to Dubai Millennium, a short-lived champion. Wherever you turn there are trophies: Frankie Dettori, Godolphin's retained jockey, has won 467 races out of 1,449. But the largest trophy in international horse racing is the 5kg Dubai World Cup, displayed at the gallery in a room of its own.

Hatta

INFORMATION

🚑 Off map at IFC 3B

Hatta Heritage Village
☎ 852 1374
🕐 Sat–Thu 8am–8.30pm, Fri 2.30–8.30
♿ Good

The mountain village of Hatta, less than 10km from the Oman border, is Dubai's oldest outpost. It's a popular spot for day-tripping Dubaians.

To reach it, simply follow Route 44 out of Dubai; it's about a one-hour drive (▶ 18). The village is a relatively lush oasis among the dusty, serrated slopes, thanks in part to a dam in the hills above. There are few attractions in the centre, apart from two watchtowers dating from 1880, but on the left of the first roundabout as you enter the village is the Hatta Fort Hotel, an attractive, 50-suite hotel with restaurants, a golf course and a swimming pool. If you're not staying overnight here – and it is the only place to stay in Hatta – then at least pop in for a chilled drink. The information centre in the lobby offers guided tours in four-wheel-drive vehicles or maps and instructions if you're feeling confident enough to drive off-road yourself.

Hatta's main attraction is its position at the trailhead for off-road routes into the Haja Mountains. Hatta's rock pools – deep, dark pools surrounded by rocky outcrops – are just a short drive away. On the way you will pass the Hatta Heritage Village, which opened in 2001. This restored mountain village demonstrates how Emiratis survived in the mountains during the last century. A fort, built by Sheikh Maktoum bin Hashr Al Maktoum in 1896 to protect against raiders and invaders, is at its heart. The site itself dates back 2,000 to 3,000 years, but most buildings are no older than 200 years. Traditional building techniques were employed, using mud for the walls and palm fronds (*barasti*) for the roofs.

Beyond Hatta the road is punctuated by ever-smaller settlements until it eventually peters out all together, and a rugged four-wheel-drive vehicle is necessary to continue.

Heritage House

Find out how Dubai's inhabitants lived 100 years ago; you'll be surprised at the changes and at the Islamic traditions that remain.

Heritage House is one of the most fully realised restorations of a traditional house in Dubai. It was built in 1890 by Mattar bin Saeed bin Muzaaina and restored by the Dubai Municipality in 1994. Room by room, the exhibition explains everyday life in a typical Emirati family home between 1890 and the 1950s. The *majlis*, or living room, is the heart of an Emirati house. It's the room for receiving visitors and, since hospitable Arab families welcomed friends and strangers alike, it is usually separate from the living quarters.

Women had their own *majlis* – a display in the Heritage House shows the household's women sewing, making Arabic coffee and applying henna to their hair. The main living room, the 'Al Makhzan', is where families meet, eat and talk together. Newly married couples, however, had the privacy of the bride room, 'Al Hijla'. Each of these displays explains what every item in the room was used for, and the museum ranks as the most informative in Dubai. To find it, take the road running parallel to and behind Al Khor Road, close to Deira's corniche.

Al-Ahmadiya School is in the alley beside Heritage House. The school was built in 1912 for the children of Dubai's ruling classes, with an upper floor added in 1920. In 1922, extra space was made for students when Islamic law, the Koran and the sayings of prophet Mohammed were added to the curriculum. Students would sit on mats surrounding their teachers. By 1963 the number of students had outgrown its premises, and the school was relocated.

INFORMATION

+ IBC 2A
- 28 Sikka Street
- 226 0286
- Sat–Thu 8–7.30, Fri 2.30–7.30; during Ramadan Sat–Thu 9–5, Fri 2–5
- Free
- Poor; steps to upper floor
- The Souks (➤ 46)

Intricate door detail in Heritage House

Jumeirah Mosque

INFORMATION

➕ IFC 2B
✉ Beach Road
☎ 353 6666
🕐 Tours for non-Muslims at
10am on Tue, Thu and
Sun with a guide from the
Sheikh Mohammed
Centre for Cultural
Understanding, a short
way down Beach Road

Jumeirah Mosque is the largest and prettiest mosque in Dubai, and it is the only one in the United Arab Emirates open to non-Muslims.

Joining the hour-long morning tour (see left) with a guide from the Sheikh Mohammed Centre for Cultural Understanding gives you a chance to admire not just the interior of the mosque, but also to find out anything you've ever wanted to know about Islam but were afraid to ask – questions are encouraged and you won't offend. But it's not a platform for proselytising and the whole encounter is gently informative.

The mosque was built in 1975 in the medieval Fatimid style, a copy of a larger mosque in Cairo, Egypt. A separate wing, behind the wooden doors to the left, is the women's prayer section – women don't worship with men in the United Arab Emirates.

The façade of the mosque has some filigree stonework, intended to add depth and warmth to the exterior. Inside, the deliberately low-key decoration has Turkish and Egyptian influences. A square arrangement of pillars supports a central, painted dome, the *qubba*, while the imam, or leader, faces Mecca from the *mehrab*, his pulpit.

There are 700 mosques in Dubai, but modern Jumeirah Mosque has a special appeal

Shoes are removed before entering the mosque as a sign of respect for other worshippers as Muslims pray and prostrate themselves on the floor. There is no physical distance between worshippers because everyone is equal: the king prays alongside the taxi driver. Male and female visitors are expected to dress conservatively, covering arms and legs, and women should also wear a headscarf.

If you miss seeing Jumeirah Mosque in person, you'll find an image of it on the 500Dh bank note.

Madinat Jumeirah

Madinat Jumeirah is to Arab culture what Disneyland is to America. The vast complex has it all – down to a specially created shipwreck.

Madinat Jumeirah is excess in all areas: part hotel, part leisure complex, it takes theming to another level. The bulk of the resort is the Mina A'Salam Arabian-themed hotel, but public areas include Dubai's only theatre and a souk. No other resort matches the over-the-top design of Madinat Jumeirah. Everything here is fake, from the windtowers to the *abras* that ply the 4km of waterways. Unless you're staying at the Mina A'Salam, a boutique hotel with nearly 300 rooms, or in one of Al Qasr's suites (some costing 30,000Dh per night), you'll be restricted to the restaurants, the souk or one of the entertainment venues, such as Dubai's largest nightclub, Trilogy, or the 442-seat Madinat Theatre. There are 70 shops in the souk shopping area. (It's not the most realistic interpretation of a souk, though, with its wide walkways and non-negotiable pricing policy.) The most interesting shops are those selling arts, crafts, jewellery and antiques – all for a price. The entrance to the theatre is also in the souk.

Outside, live-music events are staged in the 1,000-seat amphitheatre, which backs onto a waterway. Trilogy nightclub (▶ 59) is on a similarly super-sized scale; the venue is the leading night out for Dubai's party set, and many warm up beforehand in one of Madinat Jumeirah's many excellent bars and restaurants.

INFORMATION

➕ IFC 1C
✉ Interchange 4, Sheikh Zayed Road
🖥 www.madinatjumeirah.com
🍴 Many good cafés, restaurants and bars
↔ Burj Al Arab (▶ 25), Wild Wadi (▶ 47)

Browsing the arts and crafts in the souk area

Majlis Ghorfat Um Al Sheef

INFORMATION

🔲 IFC 2B
✉ Signposted from the corner of Beach Road and 17th Street, by the HSBC bank
☎ 394 6343
🕐 Sat–Thu 9am–midnight, Fri 3.30–8.30
💰 Inexpensive

Dubai's future was finalised at this modest house, where you can sit in the room where the foundations for the city were laid.

A *majlis* is a meeting place, but the Majlis Ghorfat Um Al Sheef is a more significant site than most because it was here, in the late 1950s, that discussions took place about Dubai's future. The complex was constructed in 1955 and was used by the late Sheikh Rashid bin Saeed Al Maktoum as a summer resort. The area was then populated by fishermen living in beachside shacks; today, suburban villas surround the Majlis and it can seem rather underwhelming. But the site is culturally, if not aesthetically, important: it shows how differently people lived until recently. In little more than 20 years, Dubai went from being a largely agrarian society without electricity to building its first skyscraper. Emiratis moved from windtowers to air-conditioning units, from collecting rain water to desalination plants.

The courtyard has a traditionally irrigated garden, a *falaj*. There is also a pond, a garden and a traditional palm shelter, now used to protect a soft-drink dispenser from the sun.

The two-storey building has an open-sided veranda (a *rewaaq*) at ground level and a *majlis*, complete with cushions, rugs, tea-making facilities and ornamental rifles, upstairs. The walls are made from coral and gypsum, while the doors and window frames are solid teak. In Arab architecture form follows function, and the *majlis* is cooled by a windtower, which guides cooling breezes into the room.

In the 1960s the Majlis Ghorfat Um Al Sheef was used as a police station before falling into disrepair. It was restored by the Dubai Municipality, partly to remind people of Dubai's recent past; to glimpse Dubai's future, stand on the roof to see the Burj Al Arab in the distance.

The Majlis illustrates how Emiratis lived only a generation ago

Mall of the Emirates

The largest mall in Dubai, with 400 shops, also puts children on a Magic Planet and slide skiers down an indoor ski run.

The silver, cigar-shaped extension sticking out of the palatial complex on the desert side of Sheikh Zayed Road is Ski Dubai (▶ 45), the first indoor ski resort in the United Arab Emirates, but probably not the last.

You will need more than a one-day trip to explore all of the shopping mall itself. Built on three levels, it's a town within a city. There are several entry points where you can pick up a map and plan your route. The biggest outlets are the department stores Debenhams on the ground floor and Harvey Nichols on the first floor. On the first floor you'll find the Magic Planet children's zone (▶ 50) and the supervised Peekaboo play area for younger children, close to Ski Dubai, as well as the Cinestar cinema complex.

Shops at the Mall of the Emirates cover every conceivable commodity. Men's and women's clothing represents the largest category, with a dedicated zone in the Via Rodeo for the likes of Armani, Marc Jacobs and Yves St Laurent. You can also buy homewares at about 20 stores, not to mention electronics, toys, perfumes, jewellery, accessories, books and music.

At the time of writing, Mall of the Emirates was open but incomplete. In 2007, Dubai's second theatre venue, the Dubai Community Arts Theatre (tel: 341 4777; www.ductac.org) opened, a welcome addition to the cultural calendar.

INFORMATION

➕ IFC 1C
✉ Interchange 4, Sheikh Zayed Road
☎ 409 9000; www.malloftheemirates.com
🕐 Sun–Wed 10–10, Thu–Sat 10–midnight
🍴 Many restaurants and cafés

You could easily spend days – and a fortune – sampling all the stores here

Nad Al Sheba

INFORMATION

➕ IFC 2C

✉️ Off Al Ain–Dubai road; signposted from Interchange 1 and 2 of Sheikh Zayed Road

☎️ 332 2277; www.dubairacingclub.com

🕐 Race nights Oct–Apr Thu 7pm

💵 General admission and parking free (except for Dubai World Cup race)

♿ Moderate

🔁 Burj Dubai (➤ 26), Falcon and Heritage Sports Centre (➤ 50), Godolphin Gallery (➤ 35)

Race night at the stylish Nad Al Sheba racecourse is an important social event in Dubai and also an opportunity to see some of the finest Arabian horses in action.

Race Night at Nad Al Sheba should be an essential part of any winter-time visit to Dubai. The track features a 2,000m-long turf course inside a 2,200m dirt course, running past the roll-shaped grandstand. The illegality of gambling in the United Arab Emirates has been circumvented by the giving away of prizes for correct predictions of race results.

The whole of Dubai society turns up for the World Cup races in March, and if you are lucky enough to find a space among the 50,000 spectators, it is a great opportunity for watching people as well as horses.

Horses aren't the only animals to get pulses racing at Nad Al Sheba. Camel racing has long been a favourite entertainment of Emiratis and the camel racing track at Nad Al Sheba is a hive of activity in the mornings. The season runs from November to April. A racing camel is smaller and faster than an ordinary camel and can cost several million dirhams. In the past they were piloted by small child jockeys, but this practice has been outlawed and all jockeys are supposed to be aged over 15. Radio-controlled robot alternatives to human jockeys have been successfully trialled in recent years – you can see what looks like a monkey-sized device with a rotating whip strapped to the camel's back. An operator follows the camel during the race and controls the robot with a joystick. Beside the dusty racecourse, the Nad Al Sheba camel market sells every camel-related accessory imaginable, including attractive, multi-purpose blankets.

The crowds arrive for a thrilling evening race

Palm Deira

Of the three Palm Islands being constructed off Dubai's shore, the largest is the one attached to the corniche of Deira. When completed in 2009 it will add 400km to Dubai's coast.

INFORMATION

- IFC 2A
- The three Palm Islands branch off the mainland at Deira, Jumeirah and Jebel Ali
- www.thepalm.ae

The crescent protecting the Palm from the open sea will be the world's largest breakwater at a length of 21km, while the 8.5km-wide island will extend 14km into the Gulf and use 1 billion cu m of rock and sand for its foundations, which delve to 22m below sea level. Along the 41 fronds, 8,000 houses will be built, with attendant marinas, malls, sports facilities, hotels and restaurants. Private and public beaches will line the fronds, with between 150m and 400m of sea between each frond. The entire Palm, with an area of 80sq km, will be larger than Manhattan and comparable to Greater London.

While Deira's corniche itself doesn't have the visual interest of a creekside stroll, it's where many locals promenade on weekend evenings. The Shindagha fish market, held in a car park close to the Hyatt Regency Hotel, is open daily 7am to 11pm. A museum in the marketplace explains Dubai's seafaring heritage and illustrates some of the 300 species of fish caught in the surrounding seas.

Palm Deira's sister development in Jumeirah, Palm Jumeirah, is several years closer to completion. In 2007, the property development Marine Residences was nearing completion, while the underwater tunnel connecting the island to the mainland next to the One&Only Royal Mirage resort was finished. Already villas and apartment blocks line eerily empty roads, and the venerable cruise ship QE2 has been acquired to moor here permanently as hotel and exhibition space from 2009. There's even a monorail, a first for Dubai, due in 2008.

Sheikh Saeed Al Maktoum House

INFORMATION

- IBC 2A
- Shindagha
- 393 7139
- Sat–Thu 8–8.30, Fri 3.30–9.30; during Ramadan Sat–Thu 9–5, Fri 2–5
- Inexpensive

The house of former ruler Sheikh Saeed Al Maktoum is now a museum documenting Dubai's transition from desert state to skyscraper city.

Rather than a re-creation of traditional Emirati life, which can be found in Deira's Heritage House, a more conventional approach is taken. Duck under the low doorways to find a model of old Dubai and galleries of black-and-white photographs of the city in the 1960s and 1970s.

Museum guides add greater human interest to the exhibits and provide an account of the Maktoum family's history. Originating from a Bedouin desert tribe near Abu Dhabi, the family's rags to riches story began when they moved to Dubai in the 1833 to capitalise on the sea-trading potential of the creek. From that point on, the Maktoums were constantly at odds with their ruling cousins of Abu Dhabi. This state of unrest continued until the 1950s, when Abu Dhabi hit oil. However, they were unable to import the heavy drilling equipment without coming to an agreement with the Dubai branch of the family: the Maktoums could keep Dubai if they let Abu Dhabi use it for importing the oil-industry equipment. Until this point, the Emiratis had only an oral history – nothing was written down until the 1950s. Dubai didn't even have electricity until the 1960s; yet today the tribal leaders are the CEOs of major international companies.

Restored in 1986, the house was constructed from coral covered in lime and sand plaster in 1896, the region's traditional building technique until the 1970s.

The nearby Heritage and Diving Village endeavours to show how Emiratis lived in the past. It is often not fully operational, but when staff are there, they will explain how goods were made and pearls harvested.

Elaborate door in Sheikh Saeed Al Maktoum House

Ski Dubai

With five runs, 30 tons of snow and quad lifts, the 25-storey-high Ski Dubai indoor ski slope is one of the city's most remarkable attractions.

INFORMATION

➕ IFC 1C
✉ Mall of the Emirates, Interchange 4, Sheikh Zayed Road
☎ 409 9000
🕐 Sat–Tue 10am–11pm (last ticket 9.30), Wed–Fri 10am–midnight
💰 Expensive

Even looking into Ski Dubai from the viewers' gallery at the Mall of the Emirates (➤ 41), it is apparent exactly what a technological achievement the construction is. Quad chairlifts relay skiers up to the top of the five slopes, including the world's first indoor black run. You can get a bite to eat at the all-too-convincing St Moritz Café at the foot of the hill, or the Avalanche Café halfway up. Everywhere is frosted with snow, created by what is, in simple terms, a giant air-conditioning system. Up to 30 tons of snow is made daily, covering 22,500sq m, including a 3,000sq m Snow Park. Insulation keeps Ski Dubai cool even in the summer months – the designers have described it as the world's largest refrigerator. Ski Dubai's runs are up to 85m high, 80m wide and 400m long, so there's enough space for 1,500 people at any one time.

The perfect escape from the desert heat?

Since opening in January 2006, the resort has proved extremely popular, so book ahead at weekends. It provides all equipment (except gloves) and tuition if you don't meet the minimum skills level. Lessons are in groups of up to 10 people or one-on-one with an instructor for 300Dh per hour. If you're not cut out for

skiing, there's always the twin bobsleigh track to hurtle down, or a purpose-built, snowball-throwing gallery and a 90m-long quarterpipe for snowboarders. In a city of the absurd and the outlandish, Ski Dubai still manages to amaze.

The Souks

INFORMATION

➕ IBC 3A
✉ Gold and Spice souks in Deira, Textile Souk in Bur Dubai
🕐 Daily 9–1, 4–10
♿ Good
↔ Heritage House (➤ 37)

The street markets of Deira are an exciting medley of jewellery, clothing and exotic spices. They also explain Dubai's origins as an international trading post.

In the heart of Deira's old town, the Gold Souk is a lattice of streets lined with shops selling gold jewellery. Most is of the bright, pure 24-carat variety, but you can also request 18-, 21- and 22-carat pieces. And if you don't like any of the bling on offer, a craftsman can create a piece of jewellery to your design. Some of the best souvenirs are small items such as gold tie clips or money clips. Off the main artery of the Gold Souk, a few shops sell interesting antique silver items from Oman, which are highly sought-after. Beside the Gold Souk there is a smaller Textile Souk, where you can find anything from Sinbad-style sandals, saris and pashminas to shishas and other souvenirs. The Textile Souk is where haggling pays dividends; however, gold traders don't need to lower their prices so don't expect much of a discount, except during the biannual Shopping Festival (➤ 22 and 77).

Next to the Old Souk Abra Station, on Old Baladiya Road, the Spice Souk occupies an alley alongside the perimeter road in the Al Ras neighbourhood. You can see why the souks flourished here: to one side, dhows carrying spices and other commodities crept up the creek and unloaded their cargoes on the adjacent wharf. Goods are not limited to spices; there are sacks of frankincense, camomile tea, rose petals, dried chillis and lemons, but the best buys are vanilla pods and saffron. The saffron is sold in varying levels of quality, from the cheapest (the yellow ends of the crocus flower dipped in red dye, used only for colouring food) to the finest (the naturally red tips of the stamens, best for colour and flavour).

Embroidered slippers for sale in the Textile Souk

Wild Wadi

Certainly the wettest and probably the most enjoyable theme park in Dubai, Wild Wadi is a thrilling way to cool down with the family and beats the beaches for convenience.

Wild Wadi, a 5ha theme park complex, occupies a prime position at the entrance of the Burj Al Arab island on Beach Road. This is an excellent day out, with 23 rides for adults and children, plus restaurants so you can keep your strength up. Key attractions that you might have to queue for are the Jumeirah Sceirah (pronounced 'scarer') ride, a 33m drop and speeds of 80kph on the biggest waterslide outside North America; the Whitewater Wadi, which connects to 11 water slides, and the Flood River Flyer, which connects to six slides: strong swimmers only here, please.

Visitors can enjoy the family play area in Juha's Dhow or explore the Wadi Wash and Fossil Rock; every hour, thanks to the miracle of sound and light technology, a storm breaks here, with thunder, lightning and even a flash flood. Whitewater rafting experiences are provided by the Flood River and Rushdown Ravine. If you're not scared of the dark, try running the Tunnel of Doom, an underground tube of twists and turns in total darkness.

However, the best reason to get wet at Wild Wadi is Breaker's Bay, where you can learn to surf in man-made waves of varying sizes that roll in relentlessly, and in the smaller-scale WipeOut and Riptide Flowrider waves.

The theme park is open all day, but there are reduced prices for the three-hour Sundowner sessions. Opening hours are longer in the summer, when Wild Wadi is a refreshing place to be in the sultry heat of the evenings. The park has two entrances: the main entrance is by the Burj Al Arab causeway, the other is for Jumeirah resort guests.

INFORMATION

- IFC 1B
- Beach Road
- 348 4444; www.wildwadi.com
- Nov–Feb daily 11–6; Mar–May and Sep–Oct daily 11–7; Jun–Aug daily 11–9
- Expensive
- Burj Al Arab (► 25), Madinat Jumeirah (► 39)
- Parking is limited, so take a taxi

Zabeel Park

INFORMATION

🔳 IFC 2B
✉ Zabeel
🕐 Daily 8am–11pm
💷 Inexpensive
🔄 Dubai World Trade Centre
    (➤ 33)

Take a break from shopping and sight-seeing in the city centre with a stroll around the first technology-themed park in the Middle East.

Zabeel Park cost 200 million Dh and opened in December 2005, providing a green respite from downtown Dubai. Much of the money has been spent on landscaping the 47ha park. Entry is on the north side of Sheikh Zayed Road, best accessed by taxi, although there is plenty of parking space. In this section of the park, the Stargate dome houses an IMAX screen, and the egg-shaped, 2,000-capacity Megabowl amphitheatre hosts live music shows. Children can try the Space Maze, based on the planetary system, to one side of the dome. There are barbecue areas, or you can eat at one of the food courts.

Although there's an entry fee, most attractions are free once you are inside the park. Cross the bridge, suspended from a 52m spar and 16 steel cables, to reach the southern section of the park, which is dominated by a boating lake complete with a geyser fountain and an island with its own gazebo. Pedal, rowing or battery-powered boats can be rented. On this side of the park, children can burn off energy on the assault course, or join in a game of cricket on the mini-cricket pitch. A mini-golf course is a more sedate option – clubs can be rented from the ticket office.

Adding to the futuristic feel, visitors can rent a two-wheeled Segway to get around the park (100Dh per hour). You need a sense of balance: stand on the platform and lean forwards to get the device moving. For those who decline such gimmicks, a road train chugs around the park. Creekside Park may be a better venue for a special day out, but if you're in the city centre already, it's an excellent place to spend two or three hours.

DUBAI'S
best

For Children

WONDERLAND

Wonderland, at Garhoud Bridge, encompasses a water park, Splashland, with slides and rides, and a funfair. There's a pay-as-you-go system with rides such as the rollercoaster on the right side of the park costing 10Dh a time and others, such as the pirate ship for younger children, a mere 5Dh each. However, looking increasingly decrepit, Wonderland suffers in comparison with Wild Wadi (➤ 47), the water park in Jumeirah and Children's City. Call before visiting (☎ 324 1222) as the opening times seem variable.

CHILDREN'S CITY

The building, a collection of blue, yellow and red asymmetric shapes, looks as if it has been constructed from Lego and was inspired by a children's game. Inside, the space is divided into zones themed on the human body, physical science, international culture, nature, computing and space exploration. All the displays are interactive in some way and involve some aspect of play. The auditorium can accommodate 300 people for shows, while the planetarium is the highlight for many visitors. The project, which cost 77 million Dh, has gained international recognition from the UNESCO World Museum Council.

➕ Off map at.IBC 2D ✉ Creekside Park ☎ 334 0808; www.childrencity.ae 🕐 Sat–Thu 9–8.30, Fri 3–8.30; during Ramadan daily 8pm–1am 💷 Moderate

Children's City is full of bright and cheerful characters

FALCON AND HERITAGE SPORTS CENTRE

As you exit the Nad Al Sheba camel-racing area, turn right for the new Falcon and Heritage Sports Centre. This new building, designed to mimic traditional Arabic architecture on a magnified scale, houses shops and a tented exhibition space dedicated to falconry and other traditional Arab sports; flying displays take place outside. Falconry has a dedicated following in Dubai and birds can cost up to 150,000Dh each.

➕ IFC 2C ✉ Next to Nad Al Sheba camel-racing track ☎ 338 0201 🕐 Times vary 💷 Free

MAGIC PLANET

The psychedelic funfair at the top right flank of Deira City Centre mall is more than surface style; it delivers with a superb range of rides and games. Younger patrons can play on the Flying Tigers and Jumping Star, while older children can be strapped into the wildest ride, Equinox. Next to the escalators going up to Magic Planet is a 9m-high climbing wall. Cosmic Bowling (☎ 341 4444) is an appropriate name for the 12-lane, neon-lit bowling alley, split over three levels, while carousels, Ferris wheels, pirate ships and bumper cars add to the whirlwind of activity. Several fast-food outlets include a branch of the Johnny Rockets burger bar and TGI Fridays.

➕ IBC 3D ✉ Deira City Centre ☎ 341 4000 🕐 Fri–Wed 10am–midnight, Thu 10am–1am 💷 Moderate

Sports

DRIVING

Driving in Dubai isn't for the faint-hearted, but there are plenty of other ways to get behind the wheel and have some fun. Out of the city, dune driving has become extremely popular with tourists and locals alike. Some sightseeing trips, such as the journey to Hatta's rock pools (► 18), also require four-wheel-drive cars. But if you want to stay on tarmac, visit the new Autodrome in Dubailand for a driving lesson in a high-speed sports car around the track. If that's too much, there's always the karting course opposite.

GOLF

The emirate's first golf course opened in 1988, bringing swathes of green to the desert landscape, and seven other courses have followed, all welcoming visitors for a round. No expense has been spared: the best course designers were commissioned, original club houses, such as the sail-shaped Dubai Creek Golf Club and the Bedouin tents of the Emirates Golf Club, were constructed and hosepipe bans are unheard of thanks to water from Dubai's desalination plants. Thomas Bjorn, Colin Montgomerie and Jack Nicklaus are some of the golfers who have been involved in creating courses in Dubai.

SKIING

Yes, in this land of sweltering summer temperatures, year-round sunshine and sand dunes, skiing is the newest activity on offer. Ski Dubai (► 45) indoor slope in the Mall of the Emirates and a second ski centre being built in Dubailand have introduced snow sports to the desert.

SPECTATOR SPORTS

Dubai's government has striven to bring world-class sporting events to the emirate and it has been a successful policy. Already, the city hosts a tennis open, a golf championship, the world's richest horse race and a stage of the Rally World Cup. But the Dubailand project will attract even more (► 30).

WATER SPORTS

Ever more exciting ways of enjoying Dubai's miles of Gulf coastline are being introduced. Kitesurfing is a fast-growing water sport, with equipment to rent and lessons readily available. You can also go waterskiing, windsurfing, jet-skiing and sailing. Dubai Marina is the hub of water sports on Jumeirah, but many of the beachfront resorts organise their own activities. Offshore, visitors can also go game fishing or scuba diving, while those who prefer to explore the Arabian Gulf can hire fully crewed yachts and boats.

EMIRATES GOLF CLUB

The distinctive Bedouin tents on the desert side of Sheikh Zayed Road herald the Emirates Golf Club. The other giveaway is the luxuriant lawns of the fairways contrasting with the dusty construction sites at this end of the town, in the up-and-coming residential Emirates Hills area. Each February the club hosts the Dubai Desert Classic, one of the richest golf competitions in the world. There are two courses, the Majlis and the Wadi course, both par-72; the Majlis was the first grass golf couse in the Middle East when it opened in 1988. A floodlit driving range and putting green allow after-hours practice of your tee-off and finishing technique. www.dubaigolf.com

Tee off at Emirates Golf Club

Beaches and Parks

In the Top 25

🖪 CREEKSIDE PARK (► 28)
🖫 ZABEEL PARK (► 48)

APPROPRIATE DRESS

Beachwear (swimsuits or bikinis for women, trunks or shorts for men) is acceptable only on Dubai's beaches. Visitors to parks are advised to cover up with a T-shirt and shorts. Beachwear is not accepted in resort restaurants either, even if they are outdoors.

Relaxing at Jumeirah Beach Park

DUBAI MARINE BEACH RESORT AND SPA ($$)

The closest beach resort to Dubai's commercial heart might be showing its age, but it offers good value for money. Attractions include hot bar Sho Cho, Tex-Mex restaurant The Alamo and the riotous Cuban-style Malecon, where the main attraction is the Latino dancing rather than the cooking.

➕ IFC 2B ✉ Beach Road, Jumeirah ☎ 346 1111; www.dxbmarine.com

GROSVENOR HOUSE WEST MARINA BEACH ($$$)

The first hotel to be completed in the burgeoning marina development is a tapering 45-storey tower on the waterfront. Grosvenor House has a particularly strong line-up of restaurants and bars, plus beach access at sister hotel Le Royal Meridien Beach Resort.

➕ IFC 1C ✉ West Marina Beach, Sheikh Zayed Road ☎ 399 8888; www.grosvenorhouse-dubai.com

JUMEIRAH BEACH PARK ($)

This pay-to-enter beach is definitely worth the 5Dh fee. The park gets very busy at weekends with locals enjoying the 1km sandy beach, playing games in the gardens or cooking at the barbecues. Food and drink is also sold from a number of kiosks. Lifeguards patrol the beach from early morning to sunset; swimming is not permitted after this time.

➕ IFC 2B ✉ Beach Road, Jumeirah ☎ 349 2111 🕙 Daily 8am–11pm; Mon women only 🎟 Inexpensive. Additional fee for sunbeds and parasols

AL MAMZAR BEACH PARK

In an urbanised area, the 90ha Al Mamzar Beach Park is a pleasant open space offering four beaches and several green swathes of land, chalets, barbecue and picnic areas and playgrounds. Both swimming pools have lifeguards and changing facilities and there are also changing rooms at the beaches. For visitors staying in Deira, Al Mamzar is a better option for relaxing outdoors than braving the traffic to cross the creek for Creekside or Zabeel parks. It's best to come by taxi.

➕ IFC 3A ✉ Beyond Al Hamriya Port ☎ 296 6201 🕙 Daily 8am–11pm, Wed women only 🎟 Inexpensive. Chalets extra

LE MERIDIEN MINA SEYAHI BEACH RESORT AND MARINA ($$$)

The friendly Mina Seyahi owns one of the largest stretches of private beach and has its own 238-berth marina. Guests have free use of all non-motorised

water sports, including windsurfing and kayaking.
With just 211 rooms, guests get a personal service.
You'll pay a little extra for a sea view.

🕂 IFC 1C ✉ Al Sufouh Road ☎ 399 3333; www.lemeridien-minaseyahi.com 📖 Expensive; cheaper Sun–Wed

OASIS BEACH HOTEL ($$)

Sandwiched between the Sheraton and Hilton beach
resorts, the Oasis is the least expensive resort on this
stretch of sand, but it stands up well to its luxurious
neighbours. Children have their own swimming pool
(the adults' pool has a swim-up bar). Competition for
a room is fierce – get in early. The Oasis Beach Hotel's
reputation for good value extends to its beach pass
for non-guests, costing 85Dh for adults (children
under 12 half price). On Fridays visitors can enjoy a
barbecue and beach access for 160Dh. Water sports
such as water-skiing and windsurfing are available for
an extra fee.

🕂 IFC 1C ✉ Al Sufouh Road ☎ 399 4444;
www.jebelali-international.com

THE RITZ-CARLTON ($$$)

The Ritz-Carlton is a family-friendly resort hotel with
kids' play areas in the landscaped gardens, a
supervised kids' room (ages 4–12 years) and an outdoor
pool with slides. There's building work behind the
hotel, but staff work hard to minimise discomfort.
Non-guests can use the private beach and water sports
are available.

🕂 IFC 1C ✉ Al Sufouh Road ☎ 399 4000; www.ritzcarlton.com
📖 Expensive; hotel guests only on Fridays

SAFA PARK

The emphasis in Safa Park is on fun, with bumper
cars, trampolines, an obstacle course and a small Ferris
wheel. More conventional activities are also possible
(volleyball, football, basketball and tennis), and you
can rent bicycles to get around. Several play areas for
children mean the park is very popular with families
and weekends can get busy.

🕂 IFC 2B ✉ Al Wasl Road ☎ 349 2111 🕐 Daily 8am–11pm, Tue
women only 📖 Inexpensive. Activities and bicycle rental extra

SHERATON JUMEIRAH BEACH RESORT AND
TOWERS ($$–$$$)

The Sheraton, refurbished in 2003, is popular with
European holidaymakers who appreciate its good
value. Families with children are looked after
especially well. Facilities include a freshwater
swimming pool, a gym, squash and tennis courts and
eight eateries. Access to the Sheraton's beach is free
for guests at the city's other Sheraton hotels, but
otherwise visitors have to pay. Children can use the
Pirates Club, which is supervised. Water sports are
available for adults.

🕂 IFC 1C ✉ Al Sufouh Road ☎ 399 5533; www.sheraton.com
📖 Expensive; cheaper Sat–Wed

BIKINIS ON THE BEACH

Women should note that
wearing normal Western
swimwear on Dubai's public
beaches is likely to attract
attention from local men.
Visitors may prefer to stay on
private beaches at hotels to
escape this sort of notice.

Spas

TREATMENTS

Every conceivable treatment is available in Dubai's spas, from French cosmetic treatments to traditional Indian therapies. Expect to spend Dh100–300 per treatment; a cost-effective option is to opt for the one-day or half-day packages that many spas offer during non-peak times.

Ritz-Carlton Hotel

Relaxation room at the Givenchy Spa

1847

One for the men: shaves, manicures and facials are administered in a men-only beauty parlour in the Emirates Towers' mall. You can just get your shoes shined if the hands-on treatments don't appeal.

➕ IFC 2B ✉ Emirates Towers Boulevard ☎ 330 1847; www.1847.ae ⏰ Daily 8am–10pm

AMARA

Each room at this Moroccan-themed resort has a private garden with a refreshing rain shower. The spa also has a 25m swimming pool.

➕ Off map at IBC D3 ✉ Park Hyatt Dubai ☎ 602 1234; www.dubai.park.hyatt.com ⏰ Daily 9am–10pm

CLEOPATRA'S SPA

The theme at this spa is ancient Egypt, although the hammam-like wet room has Mediterranean influences. Guests can access the lush environs of the Pharaoh Club's swimming pool.

➕ IFC 2B ✉ Wafi City ☎ 324 7700; www.waficity.com ⏰ Women: Sat–Thu 9–8, Fri 10–8; men (separate door): Mon–Sat 10–10, Sun 10–7

EL ALSALLA SPA

This Moroccan-style spa, in the members-only Dubai Ladies Club, is a relaxing place to enjoy a wide variety of spa treatments, including traditional Arabic treatments in the spa's hammam (steam room). It is one of the few spas to accept under-16s. Non-residents will have to pay an entry fee to the club on top of the treatment prices.

➕ IFC 2B ✉ Dubai Ladies Club, Jumeirah Beach Road ☎ 349 9922; www.dubailadiesclub.com ⏰ Daily 9–9

GIVENCHY SPA

This minimalist spa uses Givenchy products for a variety of facials, massages and body treatments. Beyond the spa, the hotel also boasts the best hammam in Dubai.

➕ IFC 1C ✉ One&Only Royal Mirage Hotel ☎ 399 9999; www.oneandonlyresorts.com ⏰ Daily; women 9.30–2, mixed 3.30–8; last treatment at 7

THE GRAND SPA

The Grand is a private and relaxing place with candlelit rooms, plunge pools, sauna, steam room and Jacuzzi.

➕ Off map at IBC 2D ✉ Grand Hyatt Hotel ☎ 317 1234; www.dubai.grand.hyatt.com ⏰ Daily 9–9

PARIS GALLERY DAY SPA

This women-only spa in Deira City Centre mall is a

great place for revitalising weary shoppers.
➕ IBC 3D ✉ Deira City Centre Mall ☎ 294 4000 🕐 Daily 10–10

RETREAT HEALTH AND SPA

Be rejuvenated with an exfoliation at the spa in this
marina hotel. It has separate areas for men and women
and a range of treatments, including the no-holds-
barred Balinese massage.
➕ IFC 1C ✉ Grosvenor House West Marina Beach Hotel ☎ 317
6762; www.grosvenorhouse-dubai.com 🕐 Daily 6.15am–9.45pm

THE RITZ-CARLTON SPA

More than 40 different Balinese or European
treatments are offered at this Balinese-style spa,
including the five-hour Eastern Delight package of a
Javanese full-body treatment, a traditional Balinese
facial and Indonesian scalp treatment.
➕ IFC 1C ✉ The Ritz-Carlton Hotel, Al Sufouh Road ☎ 318 6184;
www.ritzcarlton.com 🕐 Daily 6am–10pm

SATORI

Advance booking is essential at this small but relaxing
and private (guests and beach club members only) spa,
with an interior oriental garden.
➕ IFC 2B ✉ Jumeirah Beach Club Resort, Beach Road ☎ 310 2759;
www.jumeirahbeachclub.com 🕐 Daily 9–9

SENSASIA URBAN SPA

One of a handful of spas not found in a luxury hotel,
SensAsia Urban Spa is stylish and highly regarded
among Jumeirah locals.
➕ IFC 2B ✉ The Village Mall, Beach Road, Jumeirah ☎ 349 8850;
www.sensasiaspas.com 🕐 Sat–Thu 10–10, Fri noon–9

SOFTOUCH SPA

For an Ayurvedic spa experience, head to the exclusive
Kempinski Hotel, where the Softouch wellness centre
offers a variety of traditional Indian treatments.
➕ IFC 1C ✉ Kempinski Hotel, Mall of the Emirates ☎ 341 0000;
www.kempinski-dubai.com 🕐 Daily 9am–10pm

TALISE

Replacing the highly regarded Six Senses spa at
Madinat Jumeirah, Talise has a lot to live up to, but it
is already one of the most luxurious palaces of
pampering in the city. There's substance to the style
too: you receive nutritional advice and fitness
programmes.
➕ IFC 1C ✉ Madinat Jumeirah ☎ 366 6818;
www.madinatjumeirah.com 🕐 Daily 9am–10pm

WILLOW STREAM SPA

A Greco-Roman themed spa offering a steam room,
Jacuzzi and two pools: expect marble pillars, mosaics
and candles.
➕ IFC 2B ✉ Fairmont Hotel, Sheikh Zayed Road ☎ 332 5555;
www.fairmont.com 🕐 Daily 10–10 for spa treatments; 6am–midnight
for fitness

HOTEL SPAS

Dubai's spas are typically of a
very high standard, with those
in the five-star hotels leading
the way. However, these spas
may charge extra fees for non-
guests on top of the cost of the
individual treatments, and
guests at the hotel tend to get
priority for bookings. There
are several recommended
spas outside the hotels, and
these tend to be preferred by
Dubai residents.

*Go back in time at the
Willow Stream Spa*

Views

DESERT PHOTOGRAPHY

Photographers often talk about waiting for the 'golden hour' – that hour of mellow light before sundown or just as the sun is rising. This tip is particularly useful in places close to the equator, like Dubai, where the overhead sun is painfully bright and will cause bleached-out photographs. Another tip is to use a polarising filter on your lens; this will enhance the blue of the sky.

THE BOARDWALK RESTAURANT
Watch the activity on the creek from the terrace of this bar-restaurant at the Dubai Creek Yacht Club (➤ 62).

BURJ DUBAI
When the world's highest building opens, there will be viewing platforms at several levels, and you're guaranteed to be able to see for miles. For those who get seasick, note that the top of the tower is designed to sway in the wind (➤ 26).

CREEKSIDE PARK CABLE CAR
Take a cable ride to see the Dubai Creek Golf Club and Park Hyatt Dubai from across the creek (➤ 28).

HOT-AIR BALLOON
See Dubai from the sky (➤ 78).

JEBEL HAFEET
Get a bird's-eye view of Al Ain, the Garden City, from the top of the United Arab Emirates' highest mountain (➤ 15).

AL MANSOUR DHOW
Get a night-time view of Deira and Bur Dubai from a dhow cruise on the creek (➤ 62).

PIERCHIC RESTAURANT
Look back on the Jumeirah shore from this romantic restaurant (➤ 60).

SHANGRI-LA HOTEL
The pool area offers the perfect view of the Burj Dubai as it enters the clouds (➤ 71).

SKYVIEW BAR IN THE BURJ AL ARAB
For views of The World development, Madinat Jumeirah and all along the beach (➤ 83).

Abras on Dubai Creek at sunset

Desert Activities

DESERT HORSE-BACK RIDING

Camels aren't the only four-legged creature on which you can explore the desert – horse-back riding offers more experienced riders an exciting alternative to the rhythmic swaying of a camel ride.

DESERT SAFARIS

Safaris can include a number of activities and there are many operators offering a variety excursions from half-day to overnight trips. Many involve camel rides, Bedouin camps and belly dancers, as well as observing animals in their natural habitat. The largest nature reserve in the emirate is the Dubai Desert Conservation Reserve, a 225sq km expanse of desert populated by indigenous plants and animals, including 260 scimitar-antlered oryx, 4 types of gazelle and 40 bird species. The reserve opened in 1998, but to visit you will have to book a stay at the associated and expensive resort, Al Maha; one or two nights will be enough to explore the desert (check out www.ddcr.org and www.al-maha.com).

DUNE DRIVING

Dune driving is a popular weekend pursuit with locals and tourists heading out into the desert in four-wheel-drive vehicles to power up and down dunes. For those who prefer to get closer to the action, you can tear up the sand on quad bikes or dune buggies. If you're more of back-seat driver, then catch the prologue show to the Desert Challenge, a six-day desert rally for motorbikes, trucks and four-wheel-drive cars which starts in early November www.uaedesertchallenge.com.

SAND BOARDING

One new sport is sand boarding. It uses similar techniques to the more established snow boarding and attracts a similar crowd of enthusiasts. If you prefer your boarding to be on the white stuff then take a trip to Ski Dubai (➤ 45).

WADI BASHING

'Wadi' refers to the dry, seasonal riverbeds that wind their way through the Hajar mountain range; while the 'bashing' refers to the the exhilarating off-road driving that takes place along them – although some would say it's the passengers that get bashed about.

DESERT DRIVING

There are some basic rules for driving in the desert:
• Never venture off-road alone.
• Always pack sufficient water, a shovel and a tow rope in case one of the vehicles becomes stuck.
• Tyre pressures should be low: about 18psi for driving on sand, so they don't sink as deeply into the sand.
• Drive at low speeds: no more than 30kph.
• When driving on sand dunes avoid dunes with sharp ridges because these are freshly made and will be soft.
• Dunes with closely spaced ripples are usually harder than those with widely spaced ripples.
• If you start to slide, steer in the direction of the slide.

If you can ride, try a horse-back safari to explore the desert

57

Nightlife

THE WEEKEND

With the Arab world's weekend falling on Friday and Saturday (Friday is the holiest day of the week, with most shops and venues closing for at least the morning), the liveliest nights of the week in Dubai are Thursday and Friday.

THE APARTMENT LOUNGE AND CLUB

The Apartment is a new, multipurpose venue in the wave-shaped Jumeirah Beach Hotel; light snacks and cocktails are served before you hit the dance floor. Admittance is for over-21s only. Be warned: Wednesday is 80s night.

➕ IFC 2B ✉ Jumeirah Beach Hotel ☎ 406 8999; www.jumeirahbeachhotel.com 🕐 Tue–Sat 8–3

BAHRI BAR

Marvel at the views of the Burj Al Arab – and the mock-Arabic Madinat complex – from this Arabian-themed bar in Madinat Jumeirah. You can sprawl on cushions while trying Arabic sweets and some decidedly non-Arabic cocktails. There is live jazz after 9.30 most nights.

➕ IFC 1C ✉ Mina A'Salam, Madinat Jumeirah ☎ 366 6730; www.madinatjumeirah.com 🕐 Daily noon–2am

BARASTI BAR

The Barasti has the magic mix of being fashionable but at the same time unpretentious, and is in the little black book of every hip bar-hopper in town. Enjoy a shisha smoke as you watch the sun set.

➕ IFC 1C ✉ Le Meridien Mina Seyahi Resort, Al Sufouh Road ☎ 399 3333 🕐 Daily 11am–2am

The Irish Village is a lively and friendly place

BUDDHA BAR

The Buddha Bar is a seductive venue furnished with red lanterns and a giant Buddha statue. Thai food is served, but it's the cocktail list that deserves the closest attention. Later in the evening the music becomes livelier and the focus switches to the bar.

➕ IFC 1C ✉ Grosvenor House West Marina Beach ☎ 399 8888; www.buddha-bar.com 🕐 Mon–Fri noon–2am, Sat–Sun noon–3am

CIN CIN

Cin Cin is Dubai's top bar for oenophiles, with a collection of some 280 wines, from South African sauvignon blanc for 35Dh per glass to 40,000Dh for a bottle of 1982 Château Lafite-Rothschild.

➕ IFC 2B ✉ The Fairmont ☎ 332 5555; www.fairmont.com 🕐 Daily 6pm–2am

THE IRISH VILLAGE

You can enjoy a pint of Guinness at an outdoor table here. The Irish Village pub also has a craft shop and is next to a larger entertainment complex called Century Village.

+ IFC 3B ⊠ Dubai Tennis Stadium, 31st Street ☎ 282 4750;
www.theirishvillage.ae ⏰ Fri–Tue 11am–1.15am, Wed–Thu
11am–2.15am

JAMBASE

Jambase is the most consistent live music venue at this
end of town, with an in-house band playing jazzy
music. Enjoy a drink and a dance here before heading
upstairs to Trilogy. Over 21s only with a smart casual
dress code.

+ IFC 1C ⊠ The Souk, Madinat Jumeirah ☎ 366 6730;
www.madinatjumeirah.com ⏰ Daily 7pm–2am

MADINAT THEATRE

The performing arts are not one of Dubai's strong
suits; aside from outdoor amphitheatres, this is the
only venue for drama, and dance to stand-up comedy.
The 442-seat theatre is very capable though, with good
sight lines and acoustics. Times and prices vary.

+ IFC 1C ⊠ The Souk, Madinat Jumeirah ☎ 366 6546;
www.madinattheatre.com

THE PEPPERMINT CLUB

Now refurbished, Dubai's hippest nightclub returns to
dominate Friday nights, hosting top international DJs,
with the emphasis on
uncompromising house,
techno and trance sets.

+ IFC 2B ⊠ Basement of
Fairmont Hotel, Sheikh Zayed Road
☎ 332 0037; www.peppermint-
club.com ⏰ Fri 10–3

QD'S

Winter is the perfect time
to sit outside at this smart
creekside bar and watch
the sun go down.

+ Off map at IBC 3D ⊠ Dubai
Creek Yacht Club ☎ 295 6000;
www.dubaigolf.com ⏰ Daily
6pm–2am

RACE NIGHT

Race Night at Nad Al Sheba is an essential part of
any winter visit to Dubai. Don't worry, it won't be
expensive because general admission and parking is
free and gambling is forbidden.

+ IFC 2C ⊠ Nad Al Sheba Racecourse ☎ 332 2277;
www.dubairacingclub.com ⏰ Oct–Apr Thu 7pm

TRILOGY

With a capacity of 2,000 people and three floors of
dance music from a line-up of top DJs, Trilogy is a
great place to party. Rooftop Bar offers great views and
an escape from the dance floors.

+ IFC 1C ⊠ The Souk, Madinat Jumeirah ☎ 366 6730;
www.madinatjumeirah.com ⏰ Mon–Sat 9pm–3am

ALCOHOL

You will have noticed that all
Dubai's bars and clubs are in
hotel complexes. This is
because these are the only
places licensed to sell alcohol.
Dubai treads a thin line
between welcoming Western
tourists and their boozy habits
and respecting the Islamic
tenets of abstinence. There are
a few ground rules. Do not
consume alcohol in the streets
or behave drunkenly outside
nightspots. Once inside a bar,
you will find all forms of
alcohol widely available – just
don't expect a bottle of
imported wine to be cheap.

*A night at the races is an
enjoyable experience*

Places to Have Lunch

The pleasant courtyard of the Basta Art Café

APRES ($$)

Yes, an après-ski restaurant in a shopping mall in a desert – it doesn't get any weirder, but this is Dubai. Your attention may be diverted from the slopes by the excellent drinks list and some good main courses.
✚ IFC 1C ✉ Mall of the Emirates ☎ 341 2575 🕓 Daily 10am–1am

BASTA ART CAFÉ ($)

Basta Art Café is an essential pitstop on any tour of old Bur Dubai. Super snacks, such as the souk salad of couscous, chicken, cashew and lettuce, seem perfectly matched to the tranquil surroundings. The juice bar serves blends such as lime and lychee.
✚ IBC 2B ✉ Al Musalla-Al Fahid roundabout, Bastakiya ☎ 353 5071 🕓 Daily 10–10

BUSSOLA ($$$)

Sea views, soft music and a choice of 32 pizzas add to the appeal of this candlelit Italian restaurant, which has an open-air veranda.
✚ IFC 1C ✉ Le Meridien Mina Seyahi, Al Sufouh Road ☎ 399 3333 🕓 Daily 9am–midnight

CAFÉ ARABESQUE ($$)

The buffet at the Park Hyatt Hotel is a good spot on the Deira bank of the creek for a meal with a view.
✚ Off map at IBC 3D ✉ Park Hyatt Dubai ☎ 602 1234 🕓 Daily 6.30am–midnight

THE LIME TREE CAFÉ ($)

This Dubai favourite is stylishly decorated with lime-green walls and dark wood furniture. The menu has a Mediterranean slant, but there are also great cakes and fresh juices to enjoy.
✚ IFC 2B ✉ Near Jumeirah Mosque, Beach Road ☎ 349 8498 🕓 All day

PIERCHIC ($$$)

In a city of stunning restaurants, Pierchic makes a bid for the top table, with a romantic location at the end of a pier stretching from Al Qasr's beach. The Mediterranean cuisine is excellent too.
✚ IFC 1C ✉ Al Qasr, Madinat Jumeirah ☎ 366 6730 🕓 Daily 12–3, 7–11.30

SHABESTAN ($$)

Iranian restaurant Shabestan serves aromatic breads, kebabs and other Persian classics. Live music adds to the Arabic experience, and the interior has a lavish sultan's palace theme.
✚ IBC 3B ✉ Radisson SAS Hotel, Deira Creek, Baniyas Road ☎ 222 7171 🕓 Daily 12.30–3.15, 7.30–11.15

There are many places in Dubai to enjoy a light alfresco lunch

DUBAI
where to...

Deira

PRICES

Approximate prices for a three-course meal for one, without drinks or service:
$ = under 75Dh
$$ = 75–150Dh
$$$ = 150–600Dh

DHOW DINING

When the sun goes down a small flotilla of converted dhows turn on their lights and welcome aboard diners for an evening cruise up and down the creek (typically to the mouth and back). These evening trips are a great way to see the old part of the city operating as as it might have done decades ago, with trading dhows unloading goods – except the skyline is definitely 21st century. For the all-in price expect a modest buffet and perhaps a bottle of wine. The Al Mansour dhow is one of the best of the bunch, but there are plenty to choose from moored along the Deira side of the creek.

BLUE ELEPHANT ($$)

This Thai restaurant has elaborate décor – you cross a bridge over a carp pond to get to your table – and the food works well.
✉ Al Bustan Rotana Hotel, Casablanca Road, Garhoud
☎ 283 0000;
www.blueelephant.com ⏰ Daily noon–3, 7–11.30

THE BOARDWALK ($$)

The Boardwalk serves hit-and-miss meals in an idyllic setting on the creek. Sit outside to watch cabin cruisers and *abras* chug past. This place comes alive in the evening, with ambient music and the lights of Sheikh Zayed Road sparkling in the distance.
✉ Dubai Creek Yacht Club
☎ 295 6000 ⏰ Daily 8am–midnight

CENTURY VILLAGE ($$)

Century Village is a large alfresco restaurant complex behind the Aviation Club in Garhoud. There are about a dozen venues to choose from. De Gama serves a curious mix of Portuguese and Mexican dishes; La Vigna is a luxurious Italian.
✉ The Aviation Club, near the tennis stadium, Garhoud

FOCACCIA ($$)

Focaccia is a mock-rustic restaurant serving some of the city's best Italian food. The dishes are simple, but substantial, tasty and good value. A good place for a lively meal out.
✉ Hyatt Regency Hotel, Deira Corniche ☎ 317 2222
⏰ Daily 12.30–3, 7–11.30 (midnight on Thu)

LEGENDS STEAKHOUSE ($$$)

Steaks are the name of the game at this sophisticated steakhouse overlooking the golf course and the creek. Starters include pan-fried foie gras and a silky lobster bisque.
✉ Dubai Creek Golf Club
☎ 295 6000 ⏰ Daily 7pm–11pm

AL MANSOUR DHOW ($$$)

Dinner cruises on dhows are an entertaining way of seeing the creek at night, and the Intercontinental's Al Mansour dhow is the best of the lot. The food comes second to the view.
✉ Radisson SAS Hotel, Deira Creek, Baniyas Road ☎ 222 7171 ⏰ Daily 8pm departure

SHABESTAN ($$)

See page 60.

TRAITEUR ($$$)

The closest cooking gets to theatre in Dubai is at Traiteur, where nine chefs prepare modern European-style dishes in an open kitchen.
✉ Park Hyatt Dubai ☎ 602 1234 ⏰ Daily 12.30–3.30, 7–midnight

VERRE ($$$)

London-based chef Gordon Ramsay's first overseas venture is one of the most desirable dining spots in town. The modern European menu is compiled by Ramsay protégé Jason Whitelock. There's also a great, but expensive, wine list.
✉ Hilton Dubai Creek ☎ 227 1111; www.hilton.com
⏰ Sun–Fri 7pm–midnight

Bur Dubai

ANTIQUE BAZAAR ($$)
One of Dubai's best Indian restaurants, Antique Bazaar attracts a devoted Asian clientele with live music and excellent food. This is not the best place for a quiet tête-à-tête, though.
✉ Four Points Sheraton ☎ 397 7444 ⏰ Sat–Thu 12.30–3, 7.30–2, Fri 7.30pm–2am

BASTA ART CAFÉ ($)
See page 60.

BASTAKIAH NIGHTS ($$)
When the sun goes down this Arabic restaurant comes into its own. Enjoy the great-value set menu on a rooftop terrace on winter evenings. The Lebanese dishes are best.
✉ Bastakiya ☎ 353 7772 ⏰ Daily 12–12

DOME ($)
Weary shoppers refuel with coffee, cakes and snacks at this café. Décor is mock-French and the waiters play their part in black-and-white uniforms and dinky berets.
✉ BurJuman Mall ☎ 355 6004 ⏰ Daily 7.30am–1.30am

GAZEBO ($$)
Gazebo serves great Indian food with excellent service. Tandoori-cooked meats are a speciality, as are biriyanis, and you can eat well for less than 60Dh.
✉ Trade Centre Road, opposite Spinney's, Karama ☎ 397 9930 ⏰ Daily noon–3, 7–11.45

LEMONGRASS ($$)
Service is sharp in this Thai restaurant, and the food compares well with most of the city's much more expensive hotel-based Thai restaurants. But the lack of an alcohol licence means that you can't wash a green curry down with a beer.
✉ Lamcy Plaza, Oud Metha ☎ 334 2325 ⏰ Daily noon–3, 7–11

LOCAL HOUSE RESTAURANT ($$)
Curious about what camel tastes like? Find out at this traditional Arabic restaurant next door to the Basta Art Café. Main dishes are competitively priced, and don't worry, you can have chicken instead of camel.
✉ Al Musalla-Al Fahid roundabout, Bastakiya ☎ 353 2288 www.localhouse.net ⏰ Sat–Thu 10–10, Fri 1.30–10.30

PLANET HOLLYWOOD ($$)
Kids will go for Planet Hollywood's primary colours, and have their own menu to choose from. They can play games and activities during the lively Friday Brunch.
✉ Wafi City Mall ☎ 324 4777; www.planethollywood-dubai.com ⏰ Daily 9am–11pm

SEVILLE'S ($$)
For entertainment with your tapas, look no further than Seville's, where a flamenco guitarist serenades diners. On winter evenings, as the cocktails flow, the atmosphere can become positively Balearic.
✉ Wafi City ☎ 324 7300 ⏰ Daily noon–3, 7–2

SHISHA

At the mouth of Dubai Creek, in the old Shindagha neighbourhood, there are several open-air restaurants lining the waterfront. Most serve a mixture of Lebanese and Arabic cuisine, and once you have enjoyed a meal of kebabs, hummus and other local specialities, you can settle down with a non-alcoholic drink in one hand and a shisha pipe in the other for a relaxing smoke. The restaurants are of a comparable standard: Kan Zaman is a good example (☎ 393 9913), but ensure you get a table outside for people-watching potential.

East Jumeirah

ARABIC FOOD

Most Arabic restaurants in Dubai serve Lebanese cuisine. It's much tastier than traditional Emirati cooking, which tends towards the bland and basic. Lebanese dishes include favourites such as *tabbouleh* (parsley, tomato, mint, onion and crushed wheat), *fattoush* (mixed vegetables and roasted pitta bread with a sauce) and *baba ghanoush* (grilled aubergine – eggplant – dip with onion, tomato, green pepper and garlic). There are some particular flavours that are especially Middle Eastern. These include rose water and rose petals, dried fruits (from lemons to dates), pulses such as chickpeas and beans, pistachios, saffron and coriander (cilantro).

AMWAJ ($$$)

Inventive dishes flow from the open kitchen of one of Dubai's top seafood restaurants. Amwaj boasts some of Dubai's most sought-after tables, so expect prices to match; the delicious desserts, such as panna cotta with dragon fruit, sweeten the blow of the bill. Brunch on Friday offers a lavish buffet at a reasonable price.

✉ Shangri-La, Sheikh Zayed Road ☎ 405 2703 🕐 Sun–Fri noon–3, 7–midnight

THE EXCHANGE GRILL ($$$)

Revamped in 2005, the Exchange Grill's dining room can seem austere but great steaks and an outstanding wine list create a warm glow. This is one of the Fairmont's more sedate venues – for a livelier night out, head down to Spectrum On One (▶ 65).

✉ Fairmont Hotel, Sheikh Zayed Road ☎ 332 5555 🕐 Daily 7pm–1am

HARD ROCK CAFÉ ($–$$)

The Dubai branch of this world-famous café is signposted by a pair of giant guitars outside the rather anonymous building. The restaurant, on the road to Abu Dhabi, offers the familiar Tex-Mex staples of smoked chicken wings, burgers and other American classics.

✉ Sheikh Zayed Road, Interchange 5 ☎ 399 2888; www.hardrock.com 🕐 Mon–Sun noon–2am

HOI-AN ($$$)

In a convincing mock-Saigon-style dining room silk-clad waitresses serve delicious Vietnamese dishes. Starters include Saigon street-vendor soup, a clear broth with translucent noodles, chicken and black mushrooms. For the main course, charcoal grilled lemon grass chicken is a tasty, tangy choice. Hoi-An is a treat.

✉ Shangri-La, Sheikh Zayed Road ☎ 405 2703 🕐 Daily 7pm–1am

JOHNNY ROCKETS ($$)

Johnny Rockets' theme, a 1950s American diner, is superbly realised, right down to the on-table jukeboxes playing classic Americana. The burgers are excellent too, but you'll be restricted to sodas and colas since the Johnny Rockets chain is unlicensed.

✉ Jumeirah Centre, Beach Road ☎ 344 7859 🕐 Sat–Thu noon–midnight, Fri 1–midnight

LATINO HOUSE ($$$)

A steakhouse with a twist: all Latino House's dishes are inspired by South American countries, so you might find lobster and potato salad with a strawberry dressing from Colombia as a starter and an Argentinian steak for the main course. You can sit around a pool outside.

✉ Al Murooj Rotana Hotel and Suites, Al Saffa Street ☎ 321 1111 🕐 Daily 7.30–11.30

THE LIME TREE CAFÉ ($)

See page 60.

AL MANDALOUN ($$)

For a taste of delicious Lebanese food, venture into the Dubai International Finance Centre, where this superb Lebanese restaurant hides. The cooking covers all bases, including *fattoush*, kebabs and stuffed vine leaves, although it is a shame about the lifeless venue.

✉ Level 2, Dubai International Financial Centre, Sheikh Zayed Road ☎ 363 7474 ⏲ Daily 8am–11pm

THE NOODLE HOUSE ($–$$)

For fast food without fries, the Noodle House chain is a great choice. There are branches in many of the major malls in Dubai, including this one in the basement mall at the Emirates Towers. Seating is on a first come, first served basis at long trestle tables. Simply tick the dishes you would like on the menu card; noodles are the mainstay, but they are served in a variety of tasty ways.

✉ Boulevard Mall, Emirates Towers ☎ 319 8758; www.thenoodlehouse.com ⏲ Sat–Thu 10–10, Fri 4–10

LA PARILLA ($$$)

If you like your steaks cooked with a little gaucho panache, this Argentinian steakhouse on the 25th floor of the Jumeirah Beach Hotel is the best choicec in Dubai. There are tango dancing demonstrations and live music, but the chargrilled steaks are the stars of La Parilla. A children's menu caters for families, and children are welcome before 7.

✉ Jumeirah Beach Hotel ☎ 406 8999; www.jumeirahbeachhotel.com ⏲ Daily 6.30pm–1am

PRASINO'S ($$$)

This elegant beachside restaurant is a wonderful spot for a special meal. The food, from a short Mediterranean menu, stands up to the breathtaking views of the Gulf. Live jazz is played during the Friday brunch, when an extra 50Dh buys unlimited sparkling wine.

✉ Jumeirah Beach Club Resort, Beach Road ☎ 344 5333 ⏲ Daily 12.30–3, 7.30–11

SPECTRUM ON ONE ($$$)

The globetrotting cuisine at the Fairmont's buzzy but laid-back restaurant covers the four corners of the world, from the Far East to Europe via Arabia. Watch chefs at work in the eight open kitchens. The restaurant opens specially for the unmissable Friday brunch, with unlimited champagne.

✉ Fairmont Hotel, Sheikh Zayed Road ☎ 311 8000 ⏲ Daily 7pm–1am

WAGAMAMA ($$)

Wagamama, in the Crowne Plaza Hotel, is best suited to a quick, cheap meal. Enjoy a range of noodle or rice dishes at canteen-style trestle tables and benches.

✉ Crowne Plaza Hotel, Sheikh Zayed Road ☎ 305 6060; www.wagamama.ae ⏲ Daily noon–midnight

RAMADAN

Ramadan is a month-long Islamic festival, usually taking place in the autumn. For the duration of this festival, Muslims will fast from dawn to sunset. It is one of the most sacred times of the year in Islam, when Muslims will make an extra effort to avoid anything irreligious: visitors may find that restaurants close during the day and alcohol won't be served at all (although you will be allowed to consume alcohol in the privacy of your hotel room). Fasting stops at nightfall, when Muslims can be found feasting al fresco on Arabic sweets.

West Jumeirah

BRUNCH

Brunch on Friday mornings is a Dubai institution. The beginning of the Islamic weekend is the signal for visitors and expatriates to settle down to sumptuous buffets and glasses of chilled champagne at hotel restaurants across the city. The preferred spots are at beachfront hotels, but most hotels will offer some sort of brunch deal. The best venues for brunch include Splendido at the Ritz Carlton (► 67), Legends Steakhouse at the Dubai Creek Golf Club (► 62) and Mina A'Salam (► 72) in Madinat Jumeirah.

LA BAIE ($$$)

La Baie is the Ritz-Carlton's formal dining room, supplying a gourmet experience to guests and gastronomes alike. Chef Damien Chorley sends out modern European dishes with the emphasis on light and healthy courses. The restaurant opens out onto the Gulf.

✉ The Ritz-Carlton, Al Sufouh Road ☎ 399 4000; www.ritzcarlton.com
🕐 Mon–Sat 7–11

BICE ($$$)

Elegant Italian restaurants are very much in favour in Dubai, and Bice is one of the best in the city. Meat and seafood dominate the menu, although you can still order a simple, if luxurious, pasta dish. Friendly service makes the grand proportions of Bice seem cosier, but prices can be as high as the lofty ceiling.

✉ Hilton Dubai Jumeirah ☎ 399 1111; www.hilton.com
🕐 Daily noon–midnight

BUSSOLA ($$$)

See page 60.

AL HADIQA TENT ($–$$)

Several of the resorts along this stretch of beach offer Arabic-style tented areas in their grounds. The Sheraton is always popular with its guests in the evening, when an à la carte Arabic menu of *swarma* and *meze* is served to diners reclining on cushions. They're good fun for visitors of all ages although it's only the adults who finish their meals with a smoke on a shisha pipe.

✉ Sheraton Beach Resort, Al Sufouh Road ☎ 399 5533
🕐 Daily noon–3am

INDEGO ($$$)

Chef Vineet Bhatia's stellar Indian restaurant is the stand-out restaurant around Dubai Marina. You'll find it in the lobby of glamorous Grosvenor House, where Bhatia melds traditional Indian cooking to contemporary techniques and ideas to mouthwatering effect. Delicate desserts help cool the spicy main dishes. This is the best Indian restaurant in Dubai, but expect to pay handsomely.

✉ Grosvenor House Hotel, Dubai Marina ☎ 399 8888; www.grosvenorhouse.lemeridien.com 🕐 Fri–Wed 7.30–midnight, Thu 7.30–1

INFERNO ($$)

Inferno is certainly in a hot location, with an outdoor suntrap terrace overlooking the marina's yachts. This is a casual place, with the grill chefs producing Arabic-flavoured dishes.

✉ Dubai Marina ☎ 343 7710
🕐 Daily 10am–11pm

MAGNOLIA ($$)

Vegetarians rejoice! Magnolia is devoted to serving healthy, meat-free meals in the weird but wonderful setting of Madinat Jumeirah. Forget nut roasts, the dishes are rather more elegant – think risottos or stuffed baby vegetables. The

restaurant does have its own quirks, such as a menu of crystals to provide healing vibes.
✉ Talise Spa, Madinat Jumeirah ☎ 366 8888 ◷ Daily noon–3, 7–11.30

AL MAHARA ($$$)
The Burj's signature restaurant features a central column aquarium containing more than 50 tropical species, including colossal grouper and savage-looking eels. The lazier fish are hand-fed by divers, while the two sharks dine separately.
✉ Burj Al Arab ☎ 301 7600; www.burj-al-arab.com ◷ Daily 12.30–3, 7–midnight

OTTOMANS ($$$)
Have a taste of Turkish delight at this second-floor restaurant in the Grosvenor House tower. The cuisine is Turkish and Middle Eastern, and a pair of musicians playing traditional Turkish songs patrol the square dining room.
✉ Grosvenor House, Dubai Marina ☎ 399 8888; www.grosvenorhouse.lemeridien.com ◷ Mon–Sat 7.30–midnight

PACHANGA ($$–$$$)
Sizzling Latin American food isn't the only attraction on the menu at Pachanga – there's live music on every night and weekly tango and samba sessions.
✉ Hilton Dubai Jumeirah, Al Sufouh Road ☎ 399 1111 ◷ Daily 6am–midnight

PIERCHIC ($$$)
See page 60.

SEZZAM ($$)
In this vast eatery, the food is only part of the entertainment – there are often performers prowling the three culinary zones (themed around cooking techniques – steaming baking, flaming). This makes Sezzam a very family-friendly restaurant, especially for those taking a break from the endless shopping. Cuisine, like the hired entertainment, jumps all around the world.
✉ Mall of the Emirates, Sheikh Zayed Road ☎ 409 5999 ◷ Daily 11.30–11.30

SHOO FEE MA FEE ($$$)
Part lounge bar, part traditional Moroccan *riad*, this sumptuous restaurant has the best views of the faux-Arab Madinat Jumeirah complex from its terrace. The Moroccan food can be a little heavy, so choose a salad or tapas-style snacks before sinking into the cushions with a shisha.
✉ Souk Madinat Jumeirah ☎ 366 6730 ◷ Sat–Thu 7–12.30, Fri 4–12.30; drinks until 2am

SPLENDIDO ($)
With a sun-soaked terrace, views over the Gulf and a menu of simple, classic dishes, Splendido has hit a winning formula. Of course, as a Ritz-Carlton restaurant, it's still a lavish experience, never more so than for Friday Brunch (12.30–3.30).
✉ Ritz-Carlton, Al Sufouh Road ☎ 399 4000 ◷ Daily 7–11, 12.30–5, 7–12.30

THEATRICAL EATING
Bearing in mind that almost every ingredient in Dubai's top restaurants has to be flown in from abroad, dishes are never going to match the best of Paris, London or New York, restaurateurs have hit on another way to add pizzazz to a night out. Several of Dubai's leading restaurants have open kitchens, where you can watch chefs at work creating your meal. It can be an absorbing performance. Try Traiteur (► 62), Spectrum on One (► 65) or Sezzam.

Deira

PRICES

Approximate prices for a room only, not including tax:

$ = under 600Dh
$$ = 600–1,500Dh
$$$ = 1,500–10,000Dh

GROWTH INDUSTRY

The choice of hotels in Dubai is very top-heavy, with a high proportion of luxury properties where standards are incredibly high. In 2006 the occupancy rate of Dubai's hotels averaged 86 per cent, the highest in the world; this rose to 92 per cent for five-star hotels. This is despite a 43 per cent rise in average daily room rates between September 2004 and September 2005. Annual price increases have been paralleled by the number of new hotels opening: there were 416 in 2006 with a total room capacity of 35,396. Up to a further 20,000 will be available by 2010. Even so, you will need to reserve in advance for the peak period over Christmas and January.

AL BUSTAN ROTANA ($$)

An above-average collection of restaurants, the only nightclub on this side of the creek and health and fitness facilities appeal to some holidaymakers, but this is primarily a business hotel, close to the airport.

✉ Casablanca Road, Garhoud ☎ 282 0000; www.rotana.com

CORAL DEIRA ($$)

This small, Emirati-run hotel deep in Deira has facilities on a par with the big hotels. Alcohol is not available. Guests are entitled to free transport and access to the beach at the sister resort in Sharjah.

✉ Al Muraqqabat Street ☎ 224 8587; www.coral-international.com

HILTON DUBAI CREEK ($$$)

A modernist's dream, the Hilton Dubai Creek has architecture by Canadian architect Carlos Ott and catering approved by British chef Gordon Ramsay. Bedrooms have dramatic black-and-white bathrooms and, with just 154 rooms, service is personal.

✉ Baniyas Road ☎ 227 1111; www.hilton.com

PARK HYATT DUBAI ($$$)

An elegant haven on the bank of the creek, Park Hyatt Dubai has a Moorish theme of whitewashed walls, blue domes and secluded courtyards. Ground-floor rooms may have their own garden, while upper levels have balconies overlooking the creek.

✉ Dubai Creek Golf and Yacht Club ☎ 602 1234; www.dubai.park.hyatt.com

RADISSON SAS ($$)

Dubai's first five-star hotel, once the Intercontinental but now managed by Radisson SAS, celebrated its 30th anniversary in 2005. An excellent position on the edge of the creek and proximity to Deira's sites of interest attract more leisure travellers than most Deira hotels.

✉ Baniyas Road ☎ 222 7171; www.radissonsas.com

SHERATON DEIRA ($$)

The Sheraton Deira is a less expensive alternative to the Dubai Creek hotel. It's in the heart of Deira and so is a little noisier and a little less convenient for seeing the sights beyond Deira, but it is popular with visitors from Asia and businessmen.

✉ Al Matina Street ☎ 268 8888; www.sheraton.com/deira

SHERATON DUBAI CREEK ($$$)

The imposing Sheraton Dubai Creek has a good range of restaurants offering uninterrupted views of the creek. Most rooms also have creek views, as well as top-notch business services. A shuttle bus connects the hotel with its Jumeirah sibling, where guests can use the beach. The bus also drops guests off at the Deira City Centre mall.

✉ Baniyas Road ☎ 228 1111; www.sheraton.com

Bur Dubai

FOUR POINTS BY SHERATON ($$)

You can't beat the location of this mid-range Starwood hotel; Bastakiya and BurJuman are within walking distance. With just 125 rooms, the Four Points attracts a mix of business and leisure travellers.

✉ Khalid Bin Walid Street
☎ 397 7444;
www.sheraton.com

GOLDEN SANDS HOTEL APARTMENTS ($$)

Self-catering is a viable proposition in Dubai and the Golden Sands is one of the most convenient apartment complexes in Bur Dubai. You can have a one- or two-room studio, with a kitchenette, air-conditioning and a housekeeping service. Long-term stays are possible.

✉ Bank Street ☎ 355 5553;
www.goldensandsdubai.com

GRAND HYATT DUBAI ($$$)

The colossal Grand Hyatt (674 rooms and 13 restaurants in 15ha) has a running track, three swimming pools, four tennis courts and a gym. Business facilities are separate from leisure areas so guests don't cramp each other's style.

✉ Oud Metha Road ☎ 317 1234; www.dubai.grand.hyatt.com

MÖVENPICK HOTEL ($$–$$$)

The Mövenpick isn't convenient for beachgoers and the views are hardly postcard quality, but it is outside the hurly-burly of central Bur Dubai and close to several attractions and the airport.

✉ 19th Street, Oud Metha
☎ 336 6000; www.movenpick-burdubai.com

RAMADA DUBAI ($$)

Housed in a sandy-coloured, nondescript tower block, the Ramada doesn't inspire much excitement, but it offers good-value accommod-ation and is gradually catching up with its mid-range competitors by offering wireless internet, a sun deck, gym, pool and steam room. Its central location in Bur Dubai makes it popular with businessmen on a budget, and the English pub doesn't offer much for holidaymakers. However, the Ramada does have one trick up its sleeve: it has the largest stained-glass window in the Middle East.

✉ Al Mankhool Road ☎ 351 9999

XVA ($$)

This is an unusual place to stay in Dubai: eight guestrooms in an art gallery near the Basta Art Café (▶ 60) and the Bastakiya heritage quarter (▶ 24). Indeed, the XVA is in a restored traditional building; just don't expect a pool or internet access – there's a rooftop terrace on which to watch the sunset instead. Low rates mean that you'll need to book in advance.

✉ Al Musalla-Al Fahid roundabout, Bastakiya ☎ 353 5383

BUSINESS AND PLEASURE

Dubai's hotels occupy a borderland between business-only hotels and hotels for holidaymakers. Many of the hotels in Deira and Bur Dubai, and the eastern end of Sheikh Zayed Road seem intended for business travellers – the Fairmont (▶ 70) is one of the best – but they're also used by holidaymakers wanting to be based close to the old town. However, most of the resorts are located along the Jumeirah coastline, from the Jumeirah Beach Club Resort all the way down to the Sheraton Beach Resort beyond the marina. Clearly, if you want to get up and go for a swim in the sea before breakfast, these are your best bet. But if you want to do more on your break, consider one of the hotels in Bur Dubai.

East Jumeirah

East Jumeirah is the suburb where Dubai's first expat workers set up home in the 1980s. It stretches from Jumeirah Mosque all the way down to the Burj Al Arab hotel and inland towards the Nad Al Sheba racecourse.

CROWNE PLAZA DUBAI ($$$)

Most of the hotels on this stretch of Sheikh Zayed Road are geared towards business travellers, but the Crowne Plaza makes a play for holidaymakers with competitive pricing and a down-to-earth range of bars and restaurants.
✉ Sheikh Zayed Road ☎ 331 1111; www.ichotels.com

DUBAI MARINE BEACH RESORT AND SPA ($$)

The closest beach resort to Dubai's commercial heart might be showing its age, but offers good value for money. Attractions include hot bar Sho Cho, Tex-Mex restaurant The Alamo and the riotous Cuban-style Malecon, where the main attraction is the Latino dancing rather than the cooking.
✉ Beach Road, Jumeirah ☎ 346 1111; www.dxbmarine.com

DUSIT DUBAI ($$–$$$)

The two-legged Dusit is a spectacular building on Sheikh Zayed Road. It is less expensive than the Shangri-La or Fairmont but the 321 rooms are perfectly comfortable. Facilities include an open-air pool on the 36th floor, a small gym and restaurants.
✉ Sheikh Zayed Road ☎ 343 3333; www.dusit.com

THE FAIRMONT ($$$)

Often ranked as Dubai's top business hotel, the stylish Fairmont has a lot to offer holidaymakers, including sought-after restaurant tables, pool decks and the Willow Stream spa (➤ 55). Nightlife, in Cin Cin (➤ 58) and Peppermint (➤ 59), is also some of the best in the city. Service from the staff is excellent.
✉ Sheikh Zayed Road ☎ 332 5555; www.fairmont.com

IBIS ($$)

the Ibis is hard to beat for economical accom-modation. Rooms are clean, functional and comfortable, though not very spacious, and the buffet breakfast costs extra. Pleasing touches include Philippe Starck furniture and some stylish bars and restaurants.
✉ World Trade Centre ☎ 332 4444; www.ibishilton.com

JUMEIRAH BEACH CLUB RESORT AND SPA ($$$)

This bijou resort has just 50 suites, and the guests share two swimming pools (with underwater music), three squash courts, seven tennis courts, two volley-ball courts, a water sports centre and a spa. Non-members can often use the beach if partaking of a special offer, such as set brunch or spa treatment.
✉ Beach Road, Jumeirah ☎ 344 5333; www.jumeirahbeachclub.com

JUMEIRAH BEACH HOTEL ($$$)

On the north side of the Burj Al Arab, the wave-shaped Jumeirah Beach Hotel is almost as iconic a hotel. It's a vast, luxurious resort, popular with families thanks to its proximity to the Wild Wadi waterpark. Sinbad's

kids' club takes care of children while parents can hone their skills at tennis or golf. Those feeling more adventurous can also charter a yacht or take a PADI-accredited course at the Pavilion diving centre.
✉ Beach Road ☎ 348 0000; www.jumeirahbeachhotel.com

JUMEIRAH EMIRATES TOWERS HOTEL ($$$)

The Emirates Towers Hotel occupies one of the architecturally amazing Emirates Towers at the start of Sheikh Zayed Road. Predominantly a business hotel, there are good reasons for holiday-makers to stay, including great views down Sheikh Zayed Road, proximity to old Dubai and ease of access out of the city. There's a large swimming pool and health club, and complimentary access to Wild Wadi. It's the eating and drinking options that set the Emirates Towers apart: Al Nafoorah serves good Lebanese food, while the Agency (➤ 81) and Vu's (➤ 82) are famous Dubai bars.
✉ Sheikh Zayed Road ☎ 330 0000; www.jumeirahemiratestowers.com

JUMEIRAH ROTANA HOTEL ($$)

Halfway between the beach and the creek, Rotana's Jumeirah hotel is popular with business travellers but could also be a cost-effective choice for holidaymakers. The 115 rooms and suites are functional rather than lavish – but you still get a flatscreen TV and broadband. Dining options include a slightly bizarre mix of an American diner and a German beer cellar.
✉ Al Diyafah Street ☎ 345 5888; www.rotana.com

AL MUROOJ ROTANA HOTEL AND SUITES ($$$)

A pink confection on Sheikh Zayed Road, the Al Murooj has a ringside view of the Burj Dubai. Don't be put off by the impersonal, glass-fronted lobby: the 253 rooms and suites are generously sized. Two poolside venues offer alfresco dining. The Al Murooj's location allows an easy exit from the city.
✉ Al Saffa Street ☎ 321 1111; www.almuroojrotanahotel dubai. com

NOVOTEL ($$)

A slightly more refined version of the Ibis Hotel, the Novotel is for visitors who intend to get out of their hotel and see the city. Leisure travellers might like to visit the beach to have a proper swim – the pool is on the small side.
✉ World Trade Centre ☎ 332 0000; www.novotel.com

SHANGRI-LA ($$$)

This 41-storey celeb-haunt has sumptuous, chic bedrooms. Press a button and your room's curtains will open to reveal one of the best views of Sheikh Zayed Road. Guests get priority booking at the hotel's restaurants.
✉ Sheikh Zayed Road ☎ 343 8888; www.shangri-la.com

JUMEIRAH

Jumeirah itself is the one of Dubai's wealthiest districts and consists largely of low-lying detached villas commanding some of the highest rents in the city. This is the stamping ground of the Jumeirah Janes, the name locals give to the wives of Dubai's well-to-do businessmen. Accordingly, there are plenty of spas, shops and cafés along Beach Road, although the road is definitely not designed for pedestrians. While most of Dubai's new construction is taking placce in the desert or some way along the coast, developments at the Burj Dubai are focussing attention once again on this area.

West Jumeirah

HOTEL DESIGN

There is no greater concentration of luxury hotels in the world than in Dubai. But the city is also notorious for a wilful disregard of taste and restraint when it comes to hotel design. Interiors, particularly, can be disturbingly over the top – the interior of the Burj Al Arab is a prime example. However, chic minimalism isn't entirely unknown here: the Park Hyatt Dubai (▶ 68), the Shangri-La (▶ 71) and Grosvenor House (see right) are hotels that prove less is more.

GROSVENOR HOUSE WEST MARINA BEACH ($$$)

The first hotel to be completed in the burgeoning marina development is a tapering 45-storey tower on the waterfront. Furnishings are the epitome of good taste and the facilities are state of the art. Grosvenor House has a particularly strong line-up of restaurants and bars.
✉ West Marina Beach, Sheikh Zayed Road ☎ 399 8888; www.grosvenorhouse-dubai.com

HABTOOR GRAND RESORT AND SPA ($$$)

Housed in pair of towers, the large Habtoor has a prime seafront position. It may not be the most glamorous hotel on this stretch of sand, but it does everything well. Access to the Habtoor's beach costs 150Dh for adults and 90Dh for children (under 12), with prices rising to 200Dh and 120Dh respectively on Fridays.
✉ Al Sufouh Road ☎ 399 5000; www.habtoorhotels.com

LE MERIDIEN MINA SEYAHI BEACH RESORT AND MARINA ($$$)

The friendly Mina Seyahi owns one of the largest stretches of private beach and has its own 238-berth marina. Guests have free use of all non-motorized water sports, including windsurfing and kayaking. With just 211 rooms, guests get a personal service. You'll pay a little extra for a sea view. Beach access at this stylish hotel costs 100Dh (Sunday–Wednesday), 200Dh on Thursday and Saturday including brunch and 250Dh on Friday.
✉ Al Sufouh Road ☎ 399 3333; www.starwoodhotels.com

MINA A'SALAM ($$$)

Although described as a boutique hotel, this behemoth has 292 rooms, each with a sea view and a balcony. The location and setting are picture perfect and you can explore Madinat Jumeirah (▶ 39) via the man-made waterways. There are eight restaurants and bars in Mina A'Salam, and Friday brunch sessions are reputed to be the most lavish in the city.
✉ Madinat Jumeirah ☎ 366 8888; www.jumeirah.com

OASIS BEACH HOTEL ($$)

Sandwiched between the Sheraton and Hilton beach resorts, the Oasis is the least expensive resort on this stretch of sand, but it stands up well to its luxurious neighbours. Rooms with a sea view (as opposed to a view of a giant construction site) cost 700Dh more but also have a balcony. Children have their own swimming pool (the adults' pool has a swim-up bar). Competition for a room is fierce – get in early. The Oasis Beach Hotel's reputation for good value extends to its beach pass for non-guests, costing 85Dh for adults (children under 12 half price). On Fridays visitors can enjoy a barbecue and beach access for 160Dh. Water sports such as waterskiing and windsurfing are available for an extra fee.

✉ Al Sufouh Road ☎ 399 4444; www.jebelali-international.com

ONE&ONLY ROYAL MIRAGE HOTEL ($$$)

The exclusive One&Only resort has three different areas of accommodation, but even the basic rooms exhibit a 'why-not?' approach to interior decoration. Families are made very welcome, with the complimentary KidsOnly programme amusing younger children, while teenagers can learn to sail. Outside peak periods, the Royal Mirage's beach is open to non-guests – call in advance. If non-guests are accepted, access to the pool and beach costs 125Dh, but children are not permitted to use the hotel's children's facilities.

✉ Al Sufouh Road ☎ 399 9999;
www.oneandonlyresorts.com

THE RITZ-CARLTON ($$$)

The Ritz-Carlton is a family-friendly resort hotel, with kids' play areas in the landscaped gardens, a supervised kids' room (ages 4–12 years) and an outdoor pool with slides. There's building work behind the hotel, but staff work hard to minimise discomfort. Non-guest can use the private beach, but epect to pay 200Dh for adults and 100Dh for children during the week, and 300Dh and 125Dh on

Thursdays. Spaces are limited on Fridays to hotel guests. Water sports are available.

✉ Al Sufouh Road ☎ 399 4000; www.ritzcarlton.com

LE ROYAL MERIDIEN BEACH RESORT AND SPA ($$$)

Le Royal is the Le Meridien chain's most luxurious hotel in Dubai. Its 500 sea-facing rooms each have a private balcony, and facilities include a generous stretch of manicured beach, a Roman-themed spa and 14 restaurants and bars.

✉ Al Sufouh Road ☎ 399 5555; www.leroyalmeridien-dubai.com

SHERATON JUMEIRAH BEACH RESORT AND TOWERS ($$–$$$)

The Sheraton, refurbished in 2003, is popular with European holidaymakers who appreciate its good value. There are 255 rooms, most with sea views, plus rooms for people with a disability on every floor. Families with children are looked after especially well. Facilities include a freshwater swimming pool, a gym, squash and tennis courts and eight eateries. Access to the Sheraton's beach is free for guests at the city's other Sheraton hotels, but otherwise visitors have to pay 100Dh (120Dh on Thursdays). Children can use the Pirates Club, which is supervised, while water sports are available for adults.

✉ Al Sufouh Road ☎ 399 5533; www.sheraton.com

Deira

GOLD STANDARD

Dubai once had a reputation for cut-price goods. No longer: prices for clothes and electrical items in the malls are similar to those in Europe and the US. However, there are still a few bargains to be had. Top of the list is gold; it's the one commodity that remains great value for money in Dubai. Browse through Deira's Gold Souk (➤ 46) for gold jewellery. Other items that can offer good value in Dubai include made-to-measure suits, carpets imported from Turkey, Pakistan and Iran, and spices such as saffron.

DEIRA CITY CENTRE

Deira City Centre, Dubai's longtime favourite mall, is standing up well to competition across the creek. A new extension, Bin Hendi, has added the sort of marble-coated flashiness that you find in Wafi City, with a similar sort of gilt-edged shopping. Before you reach Bin Hendi, an 11-screen cinema may tempt you inside with the latest Hollywood releases. At the opposite end of the mall – and it is a long walk – the children's area, Magic Planet, will delight younger members of the family. In between lies a diverse collection of shops. Carrefour dominates the centre of the ground floor, while a Debenhams department store is on the second floor. Unlike most malls, shops of a particular type are grouped together here, so you'll find electronics shops on the ground floor near the information desk and the Arabian Treasures mini-mall on the second floor in the west court. This is where Kashmiri shawls, Persian rugs and Arabian antiques are sold. The remainder of the outlets comprise a well-balanced mix of mainstream brands and designer boutiques. Shops on the ground floor include Mothercare, Woolworths, Next, United Colors of Benetton, Zara, Diesel, The Body Shop, Nine West and the Watch House. The MAC branch is Dubai's largest and has an enormous selection of make-up. On the second floor are Banana Republic, Gap, Karen Millen, Topshop, Old Navy and Adidas, among others.

Fashionistas should follow the signs to Bin Hendi for brands like Hugo Boss and G-Star. Other names may be unfamiliar: Braccialini stocks quirky handbags; Ungaro Fever has bright, women's fashions; while Phat Farm sells hip-hop labels. Examine the spectacular diamonds at Graff from the comfort of a leather armchair in wood-panelled splendour.

Use the left-luggage office on the second floor near Debenhams where you can leave shopping bags rather than carry them around all day. The mall gets very busy at the weekends when it can be hard to find a parking space; it is better to take a taxi.
☎ 295 1010;
www.deiracitycentre.com
🕐 Sat–Tue 10–10, Wed–Fri 10–midnight

AL FUTTAIM CENTRE

This shopping complex is home to a giant Toys R Us and Dubai's first Marks & Spencer department store.
✉ Al Muraqqabat Road
☎ 222 5859 🕐 Sat–Thu 10–10, Fri 4–10

AL GHURAIR CITY

Al Ghurair, Dubai's oldest mall, is on a parallel street to the Al Futtaim Centre. Locals visit it as a less hectic alternative to Deira City Centre, but it has less to offer holidaymakers.
✉ Al Rigga Road ☎ 222 5222

Bur Dubai

BURJUMAN CENTRE
See page 27.

KARAMA
The Karama neighbourhood is just beyond BurJuman, on Sheikh Khalifa bin Zayed Road, but here, rather than pay 6,000Dh for a designer watch, you'll pay 60Dh. The shopping complex is the place to come for inexpensive (counterfeit) designer brands. The sales pitches are not overly intrusive, but show the slightest interest and you'll be badgered until you buy.

WAFI CITY
Exclusivity and variety are the watchwords of Wafi City. The mall is more compact than some of Dubai's other malls, but what it lacks in scale, it makes up for in opulence; the interior has layer upon layer of glitz and it can feel like you're in a five-star hotel's lobby rather than a shopping mall. And, with names like Versace and Chanel, Wafi City is Dubai's most designer-led emporium; it's also the home of Marks & Spencer, whose store is on the first floor.

Shops to look for on the ground floor include Chanel, Aigner and Nicole Farhi for women, while men get Calvin Klein and Pierre Cardin, among others. Meanwhile the sparkling window displays of Graff, Swarovski and Tiffany & Co. mesmerise the most jaded passerby.

But amid the diamonds and designer names, Wafi City has a handful of shops that are a little bit special. Comtesse has a sales floor devoted to Meissen pottery, some of the finest porcelain in the world, while Scarabee (☎ 324 8066; Sat–Thu 10–10, Fri 4–10), also on the ground floor, sells stirling silver ornaments. On the first floor, Wafi Gourmet (☎ 324 4433; www.wafi.com, shop Fri–Wed 9–12, Thu 9–1, restaurant Fri–Wed 10–12, Thu 10–1) is a food shop that specialises in Lebanese and Arabic cuisine, selling spices and herbs, rose water, sweets such as almond, cashew, seed, pistachio and nougat combinations, baklava and Arabic coffee.

Two clothes shops, both on the ground floor, stand out from the crowd. The boutique of Italian designer and shop owner Mariella Burani (☎ 324 5245, Sat–Thu 10–10, Fri 4–10) shows off her colourful, one-off pieces, while children's clothing shop Oilily (☎ 324 2335; www.oilily-world.com, Sat–Thu 10–10, Fri 4–10) offers an introduction to bohemian chic for the under-12s.

Take the elevator to the second floor for the Encounter Zone, which is divided into two areas, one for the under-nines and the other for older children. For more entertainment options, there's a free shuttle bus from Wafi City to the Grand Cineplex.
✉ Wafi City ☎ 324 4555; www.waficity.com

DUTY-FREE

The prices of electronics such as digital cameras and computers need to be compared carefully with prices at home, but you might make a saving at the duty-free area in Dubai International Airport. It's one of the largest airport shopping malls in the world and holds regular promotional events and competitions.

East Jumeirah

THEMED MALLS

It seems that no new mall in Dubai is complete without a theme. Two of the most elaborate are Mercato – an Italian Renaissance-style façade hiding a small but interesting selection of boutiques in a mock-Venetian interior – and Ibn Battuta, themed around the travels of a 14th-century adventurer in China, Perisa, India, Egypt, North Africa and Andalucia. But both will pale in comparison with the elaborate malls planned for Dubailand (► 30), which will include the Mall of Arabia.

JUMEIRAH PLAZA

There's an eclectic selection of shops at this pink-painted mall, including a good second-hand bookshop, a Dome café and a Dubai Police kiosk.

✉ Beach Road, opposite Jumeirah Mosque ☎ 349 7111
🕐 Sat–Thu 10–10, Fri 5–10

MAGRUDY'S MALL

Best known as a bookshop, Magrudy's carries the greatest range of titles in Dubai and there are several branches around the city. Other reasons to step inside the complex include a pharmacy, a health food shop and Gerard's – a famed patisserie where locals gather for a coffee and a pastry.

✉ Beach Road, near Jumeirah Mosque ☎ 344 4193; www.magrudy.com

MERCATO MALL

More than 90 outlets have come to this brave new mall on Beach Road, including Dubai's largest Virgin Megastore. Women's fashion is more Topshop, Mango and Next than designerwear, but men can shop at Hugo Boss and Cerruti. There's an Early Learning Centre for children. Teenagers get more choice with a Miss Sixty and Diesel outlets. On the top floor there is a mother-and-baby room, while children can play in the Fun City area. Once you've explored all the shops, there's Century Cinema showing the latest films. Note that on leaving

the mall, competition for the limited supply of taxis is fierce.

✉ Beach Road ☎ 344 4161; www.mercatoshoppingmall.com
🕐 Sat–Thu 10–10, Fri 2–10

PALM STRIP

The only open-air mall in Dubai boasts a Starbucks and a Japengo Café, plus good-value clothes shops such as Karen Millen and the Spanish fashion retailers Mango. But it's not the place to shop in the height of summer.

✉ Beach Road ☎ 346 1462
🕐 Sat–Thu 10–10, Fri 5–10

TOWN CENTRE JUMEIRAH

Beauty and skin-care products are a speciality of the shops in this small mall, which includes a Nail Station and SOS Salon. Get a foot massage at Feet First before continuing on your shopping trip.

✉ Beach Road, next to Mercato ☎ 344 0111; www.towncentrejumeirah.com
🕐 Sat–Thu 10–10, Fri 4–10

THE VILLAGE

Leave the children in the supervised Peekaboo play area while you explore some of the city's more unusual boutiques, or unwind in the sensational SensAsia Urban Spa (► 55). The Village serves the local Jumeirah community, so you will find shops that don't appear in the larger malls, such as florists, a post office and beachwear outlets.

✉ Beach Road ☎ 344 7714
🕐 Sat–Thu 10–10, Fri 4–10

West Jumeirah

GOLD AND DIAMOND PARK

There are over 60 shops in this warehouse-style business park, all selling a similar selection of 18-carat gold jewellery with diamonds and other precious stones.

Within a single store you may find that prices range from 500Dh for a pair of earrings to 500,000Dh for a set of diamond earrings, necklace, bracelet and rings. Shop around, because competition is fierce thanks to low visitor numbers – the park is a little out on a limb. You can ask for a free tour of the park's jewellery-making factory and watch craftsmen at work.

✉ Interchange 4, Sheikh Zayed Road ☎ 347 7788; www.goldanddiamondpark.com ⏰ Sat–Thu 10–10, Fri 4–10

IBN BATTUTA

No mall goes as far as Ibn Battuta in adding an extra layer to the shopping experience. Here, there are six geographical areas. Each is colour-coded and themed according to its region, so in the red-tiled China Court you'll find a full-size Chinese junk and in the purple Andalusia Court a replica of the Alhambra's Fountain of the Lions.

The tour of the world's greatest civilisations adds interest to shopping, and the colour coding and elaborate interior design, such as the tiled dome in Persia or the mosaic floors of Egypt, can help you work out where you are. Thankfully, there are

shops, as well as the 'edutainment'.

Each region is distinct but beyond the style of décor there is only a loose order to the selection of shops in each. You will find department stores, including the ubiquitous Debenhams, in Persia, alongside lifestyle outlets covering health and beauty, toys and homeware.

In the India Court designer fashion holds sway, with mainstream outlets such as Topshop alongside trendy brands such as jeans label Evisu. The Tunisia Court is home to the Géant supermarket and other food shops. Convenience and general-purpose stores are in the Andalusia Court for locals who want to do their banking etc.

Egypt has a Lego store and several clothing outlets for children, sports shops such as Nike, and a Magrudy's for books and music.

The final region, China, at the far end of the mall, has Dubai's first IMAX screen. There are also seven restaurants – the branch of the Lime Tree Café is the best bet for tasty snacks and a good coffee – and a Thomas Cook office for changing traveller's cheques.

✉ Interchange 5 or 6, Sheikh Zayed Road ☎ 362 1900; www.ibnbattutamall.com ⏰ Sat–Tue 10–10, Wed–Fri 10–midnight

MALL OF THE EMIRATES

See page 41.

SHOPPING FESTIVAL

As if extra incentive was needed, Dubai's twice-yearly shopping festival (summer and winter, ➤ 22) attracts thousands of shoppers to Dubai's 50-plus malls for super-sized discounts and competitions with extravagant prizes (think Porsche and Rolex). The original Shopping Festival takes places in January, when hotel rooms must be reserved in advance, while the Summer Surprises festival (www.mydsf.ae), during the sweltering month of June, doesn't have much difficulty coaxing visitors into the city's air-conditioned malls.

Deira

FILMS

It takes a while for Hollywood's latest hit films to filter through to Dubai's cinemas. The reason? Every film has to be assessed by the emirate's film censors, who take a hardline attitude to any controversial themes or subject matter – typically this includes political or sexual content. Recent casualties of the censor include Ang Lee's gay cowboy drama, *Brokeback Mountain*, and, unsurprisingly, the no-holds-barred comedy *Borat*. Films that are released in Dubai may also be edited for language and other content.

BARS

THE IRISH VILLAGE
See page 58–59.

OXYGEN
Underneath the glitzy Al Bustan Rotana Hotel near the airport lurks this mid-sized nightclub, the only nocturnal venue on the Deira side of the creek. Famous DJs appear intermittently, with house and R&B on the playlist most nights.
🖂 Al Bustan Rotana Hotel, Casablanca Road, Garhoud
☎ 282 0000; www.rotana.com
🕔 Daily 7pm–3am

QD'S
See page 59.

ACTIVITIES

AEROGULF SERVICES
Get an unparalleled bird's-eye view of Dubai on a (pricey) helicopter tour.
🖂 Dubai International Services, Garhoud Road ☎ 220 0331; www.aerogulfservices.com
🎫 Expensive

AVIATION CLUB
This leisure club has eight tennis courts and offers lessons with professional coaches.
🖂 Tennis stadium, Garhoud
☎ 282 4540; www.cftennis.com
🎫 Expensive

BALLOON ADVENTURES DUBAI
The company's two large balloons can each carry 40 people and be booked for groups or individuals. Flights take off in time for the sunrise.
🖂 Near Claridge Hotel, Deira
☎ 273 8585;

www.ballooning.ae 🕔 Oct–May daily 🎫 Expensive

DUBAI CREEK GOLF AND YACHT CLUB
The yacht club has a large marina where visitors can charter one of the club's four motor cruisers. The 10m *Sneakaway* is a fishing vessel on which up to six people can sail into the Gulf to hook tuna, kingfish, barracuda and sailfish, while the Princess V42 sports boat is better suited to cruising the creek and the Gulf. A 6- to 8-hour cruise will take you all the way down to Palm Jumeirah island, past the Burj Al Arab and around The World offshore construction site.

The Dubai Golf Club, on the other side of the Park Hyatt Hotel, has an outgoing nine holes designed by Thomas Bjorn. The par-71 championship course is open to non-members who have brought their handicap certificate.
☎ 295 6000;
www.dubaigolf.com
Golf 🎫 Expensive; Fishing
🕔 7–6 🎫 Expensive; Cruising
🕔 7–6 🎫 Expensive

EMIRATES MOTOR SPORTS FEDERATION
The EMSF organises motorsports events in the Emirates throughout the year, from desert rallies to classic-car shows. Check online to find out what is going on when.
🖂 Near Aviation Club, Garhoud
☎ 282 7111; www.emsf.ae

MAGIC PLANET
See page 50.

Bur Dubai

BARS

GINSENG

This independent, but licensed, nightspot includes a bar, lounge and Thai restaurant. Most people come for the cocktails, especially on Tuesdays when it's two drinks for the price of one. Décor is elegant and the clientele dress to impress.
✉ Planet Hollywood complex, Wafi City, Umm Hurair ☎ 324 8200; www.ginsengdubai.com
🕐 Fri–Wed 7–2, Thu 7–3

GOODFELLAS

A loud sportsbar screening non-stop football and rugby matches, Goodfellas is where Dubai's locals come for their fix of British football. Food and drink is equally British, beer and pies being the order of the day. Happy hour lasts considerably longer than an hour.
✉ Regal Plaza Hotel ☎ 355 6633 🕐 Daily noon–3am

JIMMY DIX

An unpretentious place to party. Jimmy Dix's reputation for back-to-basics drinking and dancing means that it is not the venue for the more discerning clubber.
✉ Mövenpick Hotel, Oud Metha ☎ 336 8800 🕐 Daily 7–3

MAHARLIKA'S CLUB

Maharlika's is the venue of choice for fans of punky cover bands and wild nights out. It's where Dubai's lively Filipino community come to let their hair down. Hard rock classics are put through an East Asian blender [by

various high-energy guitar bands, while the barmen serve up punchy cocktails.
✉ President Hotel, Trade Centre Road, Karama ☎ 334 6565
🕐 Daily 8–3

MIX

With three floors, a live music room and a lounge area, MIX is one of Dubai's largest nightclubs and there is no cover charge for entry. A less-than-full night can be an anticlimax but when an international DJ is booked get ready to queue.
✉ Grand Hyatt Hotel, Oud Metha Road ☎ 317 1234; www.dubai.grand.hyatt.com
🕐 Sun–Fri 9–3

VINTAGE

A cosy wine bar with an endearing lack of snobbery. The wine list covers most of the world – but unlike bars such as Cin Cin, Vintage is about having fun. The proof? Weekend fondue nights.
✉ Pyramids, Wafi City ☎ 324 4100 🕐 Fri–Wed 6–1.30, Thu 4–2

CINEMAS

GRAND CINEPLEX

Make a day of it at this enormous 12-screen cinema complex close to Wafi City mall and Creekside Park.
✉ Umm Hurair, near Grand Hyatt Hotel ☎ 324 2000; www.grandcinemas.com
💵 Moderate

GALLERIES

MAJLIS GALLERY

The Majlis Gallery accommodates the work

THE INTERNET

The internet hasn't escaped censorship from Dubai's authorities either. All internet services in the emirate are provided by Etisalat, a government company, and websites are monitored and restricted. Regardless, internet access is widely available in hotels and some coffee shops, such as branches of the Coffee Bean and Tea Leaf.

THE BAR SCENE

Dubai's bar scene changes faster than a dancer between songs. Today's hip bar will be tomorrow's has-been, although some places are so swanky they seem to be immune from this syndrome. For the very latest tips on what's hot or not, use an online listings directory or the Wednesday entertainment supplement of the *Gulf News*.

of both local and international artists, with a mix of paintings, sculpture, fabric printing and even furniture.
✉ Al Musalla-Al Fahid roundabout, Bastakiya ☎ 353 6233; www.majlisgallery.com
⏰ Sat–Thu 9.30–8

XVA

The artists featured in this restored windtower behind the Majlis Gallery are a varied bunch. You might catch an exhibition on Dubai's 'vertical world' or a sculpture show.
✉ Al Musalla-Al Fahid roundabout, Bastakiya ☎ 353 5383; www.xvagallery.com
⏰ Sat–Thu 9am–10pm, Fri 9–6

ACTIVITIES

BLUESAIL DUBAI

Bluesail can organise anything nautical from one-hour trips to week-long yacht charters. They have two speedboats, two 42ft yachts and three motor cruisers; crews can be provided.
✉ Al Seef Road, opposite British Embassy ☎ 374 5145; www.bluesailyachts.com
💷 Yacht charter from 4,000Dh per half-day, speedboat charter from 250Dh per hour (max six passengers)

AL BOOM TOURIST VILLAGE

Nine dhows set off from Al Boom every evening; prices include onboard dining, but the out-of-the-way location means you will also have to pay for a taxi to your hotel.
✉ Umm Hurair, next to Garhoud Bridge ☎ 324 3000; www.alboom.ae ⏰ Late-night

cruises 10.30pm–midnight
💷 Moderate

DUBAI WATERSPORTS ASSOCIATION

Beyond the dhow-building yard near Creekside Park, the DWSA provides wakeboard or waterskiing lessons in the creek. Non-members have to pay a small entry fee.
✉ Al Jaddaf ☎ 324 1031; www.dwsa.net ⏰ Non-members moderate

HOUSE OF CHI AND HOUSE OF HEALING

Tai chi, yoga, shiatsu, reiki and pilates are offered at this oriental alternative health centre. There's a choice of oriental massages, or take a martial arts class.
✉ 6th Floor, Al Musalla Towers, Khalid Bin Walid Street ☎ 397 4446; www.hofchi.com
💷 Treatments expensive

AL NASR LEISURELAND

Leisureland is an ageing complex with a bowling alley, ice-skating rink and tennis and squash courts.
✉ Umm Hurair Road, Oud Metha, near the American Hospital ☎ 337 1234; www.alnasrll.com
💷 Inexpensive

PURSUIT GAMES

Let off steam with a paintball gun and a bagful of paintball pellets. This paintballing operator in Dubai has a good safety record and up-to-date kit.
✉ Wonderland, near Creekside Park ☎ 050 651 4583; www.paintballdubai.com
💷 Expensive

East Jumeirah

BARS

THE AGENCY

Like Vu's and Harry Ghatto's, the Agency is in the Jumeirah Emirates Towers hotel. The Agency serves wine and tapas, making it an ideal precursor to more drinks at Vu's, followed by a karaoke session at Harry Ghatto's. There are definitely livelier places to along Sheikh Zayed Road, but it is fine for a quiet glass of wine.

✉ Jumeirah Emirates Towers Hotel ☎ 319 8088; www.jumeirahemiratestowers.com ◷ Sun–Thu noon–midnight, Fri–Sat 3–3

BOUDOIR

You'll need to be smartly dressed and preferably in a mixed group to get past the bouncers at this exclusive club. Once inside, the interior has a *fin-de-siècle* decadence; enjoy starlit nights in the outdoor area to a slick soundtrack. Monday night is jazz night and ladies enjoy free champagne on Tuesday nights.

✉ Dubai Marine Beach Resort, Beach Road ☎ 345 5995; www.myboudoir.com ◷ Daily 7.30–3

CIN CIN

See page 58.

HARRY GHATTO'S

The best karaoke bar in Dubai starts late and you can continue crooning until 3am. It's a compact place, behind the Tokyo restaurant, but that just adds to the atmosphere.

✉ Boulevard, Jumeirah

Emirates Towers Hotel ☎ 330 0000 ◷ Daily 8–3, karaoke from 10

THE PEPPERMINT CLUB

See page 59.

SHO-CHO

White leather furniture, large fishtanks with tropical fish and subtle blue lighting give the impression of being underwater in this trendy, minimalist Japanese restaurant and bar.

✉ Dubai Marine Beach Resort, Beach Road ☎ 346 1111; www.dxbmarine.com ◷ Daily 7–2.30

SUNSET BAR

The hotel is closed for refurbishment at the time of writing; however, the Sunset Bar will remain, though the name may change. Unlike other bars at this bijou resort, which are for residents only, non-guests can visit the Sunset Bar from 7pm, or from 5pm during special events. You can enjoy pizzas from a wood-fired oven, or take on the cocktail menu. The bar is right on the beach so expect to get sand in your shoes.

✉ Jumeirah Beach Club Resort, Beach Road ☎ 344 5333; www.jumeirah.com ◷ Daily 5/7–10

TRADER VIC'S

Head-swimming cocktails, such as Mai Tais, are the chief attraction of this Polynesian-themed bar/restaurant. Food is served in the dining area, but is spoiled by the

DRESS CODES

Dress codes for nightclubs and restaurants vary widely. Most restaurants are laidback, but will request a collar and tie clearly if they require it. Nightclubs are not so straightforward, and large groups of men in jeans and trainers can expect some scrutiny. Check in advance or ask your hotel to put you on the guest list.

smoky, raucous atmosphere; still, for a cheap and cheerful evening drink Trader Vic's remains popular. A chaotic band plays live here from time to time.

✉ Crowne Plaza Hotel, Sheikh Zayed Road ☎ 311 1111 🕐 Sat–Thu 6.30–1.30, Fri 7.30–11.30

VU'S

Take the high-speed lift to the 51st floor of the Jumeirah Emirates Towers for one of the headiest views in town: few places look as futuristic as Sheikh Zayed Road at night. This is a must-visit bar, although cocktail prices may bring you back to earth.

✉ 51st Floor, Jumeirah Emirates Towers Hotel, Sheikh Zayed Road ☎ 330 0000 🕐 Daily 5–2

ZINC

Zinc is a popular nightclub aimed at people who want to party rather than strike a pose. The music is determinedly mainstream and 'happy hour' drinks deals are generous.

✉ Crowne Plaza Hotel, Sheikh Zayed Road ☎ 331 1111 🕐 Daily 7–3

CINEMAS

GRAND MERCATO CINEMA

Located in the mock-Italian Mercato Mall, the Grand has seven screens showing the latest releases.

✉ Mercato Mall, Beach Road, Jumeirah ☎ 349 8765; www.century-cinemas.com 🕐 Sat–Thu 10–10, Fri 2–10

GALLERIES

GREEN ART GALLERY

A central player in Dubai's small-scale art scene, the Green Art Gallery exhibits original contemporary art in a large villa. Themes vary, but Arab-influenced work is often to the fore.

✉ Villa 23, Street 51, behind Dubai Zoo ☎ 344 9888; www.gagallery.com 🕐 Exhibitions Oct–May

ACTIVITIES

DUBAI OFFSHORE SAILING CLUB

The Dubai Offshore Sailing Club is a welcoming place offering private and group sailing lessons in small dinghies. It is affiliated to the Royal Yachting Association in Britain.

✉ Beach Road, by Safa Park ☎ 394 1669; www.dosc.ae 🕐 Lessons expensive

KITEPEOPLE

At the far end of this stretch of Jumeirah's shore, by Interchange 3 on Sheikh Zayed Road, is Kite Beach. With regular onshore breezes and warm water, kitesurfing is a popular sport in Dubai, but increasingly strict regulations about when and where kitesurfers can use the beach mean that they are leaving Jumeirah's main strip.

Kitepeople offers lessons to anyone wishing to try the sport and advises on the best spots.

✉ Picnico shop, Beach Road, next to Eppco petrol station ☎ 050 843 8584; www.kitepeople.net

West Jumeirah

BARS AND CLUBS

BARASTI BAR
See page 58.

BUDDHA BAR
See page 58.

JAMBASE
See page 59.

THE ROOFTOP
Kick back with a cocktail at this chilled-out bar on the roof of the One&Only Royal Mirage. Relaxation is the object here, with cushions to laze against, soothing music and views of the Burj Al Arab's technicolour lightshow.
✉ One&Only Royal Mirage Hotel, Al Sufouh Road ☎ 399 9999; www.oneandonlyresorts.com
🕐 Daily 5–1

SKYVIEW BAR
Non-guests have to make a reservation at this cocktail bar 200m above sea level. Entry require-ments are stringent: no jeans, no trainers, no sandals and a shirt with a collar for men. But it's worth the effort for the mesmerising views over the Gulf coast.
✉ Burj Al Arab ☎ 301 7600
🕐 Daily 11am–2am

TRILOGY
See page 59.

CINEMAS

CINESTAR
This 14-screen cinema in the Mall of the Emirates (➤ 41) shows Hollywood blockbusters.
✉ Mall of the Emirates ☎ 341 4222; www.cinestarcinemas.com

GRAND MEGAPLEX AND IMAX
Dubai's first IMAX screen is at Ibn Battuta Mall (➤ 77); there's another at Zabeel Park (➤ 48).
✉ Ibn Battuta Mall ☎ 366 9898; www.ibnbattutamall.com

THEATRES

MADINAT THEATRE
See page 59.

ACTIVITIES

DUSAIL
Motorboats and a 50ft yacht can be hired from this firm at Dubai Marina (➤ 31). They also offer fishing packages and two-hour sightseeing cruises, departing from the Jumeirah Beach Hotel.
✉ Dubai Int'l Marine Club ☎ 398 9146; www.dusail.com

PAVILION DIVE CENTRE
This PADI-approved dive centre offers Discover Scuba Diving sessions for first-timers and trips for experienced divers.
✉ Jumeirah Beach Hotel ☎ 406 8827; www.thepaviliondivecentre.com
💲 Expensive

PARASAILING
If you like the idea of being towed behind a speedboat while wearing a large parasail, try it at the Sheraton's beach hotel.
✉ Sheraton Jumeirah Beach Resort and Towers, Al Sufouh Road ☎ 399 5533; www.sheraton.com
💲 Expensive

SKI DUBAI
See page 45.

GOLF CLUBS

Given the amount of effort it takes, in this hostile environment, to create and keep grass golf courses in the superb condition praised by Tiger Woods in 2001, they are as good a symbol as any of Dubai's excess. If you want to test the fairways for yourself, fashionable Jumeirah has some of the best – and watch out for those gold-plated buggies.

Arabian Ranches Golf Club
Arabian, in Dubailand, is the first truly desert golf course in Dubai. The course layout, by Jack Nicklaus's design company, uses the desert landscape to present an unusual challenge to golfers. There are no water features; instead, watch out for all the sand traps! www.arabianranchesgolfclubdubai.com

Emirates Golf Club
See page 51.

The Montgomerie
This Colin Montgomerie-designed course is close to the Emirates Golf Club and introduces some of the features of a Scottish links course. The third hole not only uses the outline of the United Arab Emirates, but at 5,388sq m it is the largest single golfing green in the world. www.themontgomerie.com

DUBAI
practical matters

WHAT YOU NEED

	UK	Germany	USA	Australia	France
● Required ○ Suggested ▲ Not required — Some countries require a passport to remain valid for a minimum period (usually at least six months) beyond the date of entry — contact their consulate or embassy or your travel agent for details.					
Passport/National Identity Card	●	●	●	●	●
Visa (regulations can change – check before you travel)	▲	▲	▲	▲	▲
Onward or Return Ticket	●	●	●	●	●
Health Inoculations	▲	▲	▲	▲	▲
Health Documentation	●	●	●	●	▲
Travel Insurance	○	○	○	○	○
Driving Licence (national)	●	●	●	●	●
Car Insurance Certificate (if own car)	●	●	●	●	●
Car Registration Document (if own car)	●	●	●	●	●

WHEN TO GO

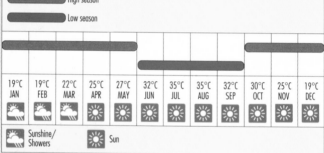

Dubai

High season

Low season

19°C JAN	19°C FEB	22°C MAR	25°C APR	27°C MAY	32°C JUN	35°C JUL	35°C AUG	32°C SEP	30°C OCT	25°C NOV	19°C DEC

Sunshine/Showers

Sun

TIME DIFFERENCES

GMT 12 noon	Dubai 4pm	Germany 1pm	USA (NY) 7am	France 1pm	Spain 1pm

TOURIST OFFICES

In the UK
Dubai Department of Tourism and
Commerce Marketing
125 Pall Mall
London SW1 5EA
☎ 020 7839 0580
Fax: 020 7287 1369

In the USA
25 West 45th Street
Suite 405
New York
NY 10036
☎ 212/575 2262
Fax: 212/826 6940

ARRIVING

Dubai International Airport (DXB) is on Garhoud Road on the Deira side of the creek, about 5km from the city centre. A new international airport is being built at the opposite end of Dubai in Jebel Ali, but for the near future DIA will be the main gateway to the city (☎ 224 5555; www.dubaiairport.com). The vast majority of flights arrive at Terminal 1.

Dubai Airport Kilometres to Dubai	Journey times
5 kilometres	🚌 N/A
	🚍 N/A
	🚗 10 minutes

New Port Ferry Terminal Kilometres to Dubai	Journey times
1.5 kilometres	🚌 N/A
	🚍 N/A
	🚗 5 minutes

MONEY

The national currency of the United Arab Emirates is the dirham. A hundred fils make one dirham, but fils are rarely used. Dirham notes come in denominations of 5Dh, 10Dh, 20Dh, 50Dh, 100Dh, 200Dh, 500Dh and 1,000Dh. There are also 1Dh coins. Credit cards are widely accepted and ATMs will dispense cash to foreign card holders. Most banks will change money without any problem. Traveller's cheques can be exchanged at currency exchanges, some banks and hotels. You will need your passport to change them.

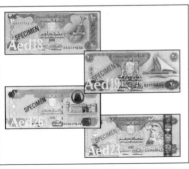

TIME

 Dubai is four hours ahead of GMT and 11 hours ahead of New York.
There are no seasonal adjustments to the clock.

VISITORS WITH A DISABILITY

Facilities for visitors with a disability are improving. There is a desk in the airport departure hall where transport around the airport can be organised. Many hotels and newly built facilities, such as Zabeel Park, offer excellent access for people with a disability.

Several organisations in Dubai are dedicated to improving access for people with disabilities. For more information contact the Dubai Centre for Special Needs (☎ 344 0966; admission@dcsneeds.ae).

CUSTOMS

→ **YES**

Customs will allow you to bring:
2,000 cigarettes
400 cigars
2kg of tobacco
2 litres of wine or spirits (non-Muslims)

⊖ **NO**

Drugs, weapons and ammunition, ivory and pearls, foodstuffs, alcohol, medical and pharmaceutical items (including some drugs legal in the west) and 'publications, photographs, paintings, cards, books and sculptures that do not adhere to religious morals'.

CONSULATES

 UK ☎ 309 4444

 Germany ☎ 397 2333

 USA ☎ 311 6000

 France ☎ 332 9040

 Spain ☎ 331 3565

TOURIST OFFICES

The Dubai Department of Tourism and Commerce Marketing (www.dubaitourism.ae) has several tourist information bureaus around the city:

Airport
☎ 224 5252 🕐 24 hours

Baniyas Square, Deira
☎ 228 5000 🕐 Sat–Thu 9–9, Fri 3–9

Sheikh Zayed Road
☎ 883 3397 🕐 Sat–Thu 9–9, Fri 3–9

Deira City Centre Mall
☎ 294 8615 🕐 Daily 10–10

BurJuman Mall
☎ 352 0003 🕐 Daily 10–10

Wafi City Mall
☎ 324 0499 🕐 Daily 10–10

Mercato Mall
☎ 344 6252 🕐 Daily 10–10

EMAIL & INTERNET

High-speed internet facilities are widely available in Dubai's hotels; many offer a wireless service. You may have to pay. There are lots of cafés where you can use the internet, sometimes for free in branches of the Coffee Bean & Tea Leaf.

Dubai's only internet service provider, Etisalat, censors the content available to surfers.

NATIONAL HOLIDAYS

J	F	M	A	M	J	J	A	S	O	N	D
3			1				2		1		1

1 Jan	New Year's Day
Jan	*Eid Al Adha
31 Jan	Islamic New Year
April	*Prophet Mohammed's Birthday
6 Aug	Accession of Sheikh Zayed
Aug	*Lailat Al Mi'Raj
Oct	*Eid Al Fitr
2 Dec	UAE National Day

*The dates for these holidays vary according to the Islamic lunar calendar and change by about 11 days each year.

OPENING HOURS

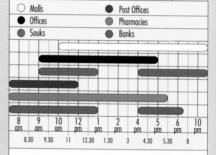

○ Malls	● Post Offices
● Offices	● Pharmacies
● Souks	● Banks

8 am	9 am	10 am	12 pm	1 pm	2 pm	4 pm	5 pm	6 pm	10 pm
8.30	9.30	11	12.30	1.30	3	4.30	5.30	8	

Friday is the holy day in the Muslim world so the weekend in Dubai is Thursday and Friday (although some businesses close Friday and Saturday instead). Most shops and other services are closed for at least part of Friday. The opening hours of banks are typically Sat–Wed 8–1, Thu 8–12. All are closed on Friday. The opening hours of malls are typically Sat–Thu 10–10 and 4–10 on Friday.

ELECTRICITY

The electricity supply in Dubai is 220/240 volts at 50 cycles.

 Sockets take three-square-pronged plugs. US-made appliances may need a transformer, but UK appliances work without one.

TIPS/GRATUITIES

Yes ✓	No ✗	
Restaurants (if service not included)	✓	10–15%
Cafés/bars	✓	loose change
Porters	✓	5–10Dh
Chambermaids	✓	5–10Dh
Cloakroom attendants	✓	loose change
Tour guides	✓	a few dirham
Taxis	✓	round up to the nearest 5Dh

GETTING AROUND

Dubai is an easy city to navigate, given that it is strung out along one main street, Sheikh Zayed Road. The older parts of the city, Bur Dubai and Deira on either side of the creek, retain narrow, convoluted routes with one-way systems. Sheikh Zayed Road has a series of numbered interchanges, with Interchange 1 being closest to Bur Dubai and the city centre, and Interchange 5 accessing Dubai Marina.

 Buses Very few people other than construction workers getting to and from work take public buses. The government is encouraging more people to use public transport with the construction of 400 air-conditioned bus shelters.

 Taxis There are 5,000 registered taxis in Dubai. For details, see www.dubaitransport.gov.ae. Drivers always use their meters but some may take you the long way to your destination. Fares are 1.5Dh per kilometre plus a 3Dh surcharge, except from the airport. Before setting off, ensure that the driver knows where he is going: some have not been in the country very long and may be unfamiliar with your destination or the route. The standard of driving of many taxi drivers is frighteningly poor. Don't be reluctant to ask your driver to slow down or pay attention if he is driving dangerously. You can book a taxi for a 12-hour day for 600Dh. Some private but licensed drivers, such as those used by hotels, can be hired for long journeys at a negotiable rate. It is customary to tip the driver by rounding up the fare to the nearest 5Dh.

 Abras Abras are the water taxis that criss-cross the creek day and night. The boats typically seat about 20 people. Official abra stations are strung along each side of the creek, generally identified by a metal sign and a large crowd of people. Abra fares are 1Dh per journey. It's a bargain.

 Metro The Dubai metro is finally underway after having been approved in 2005. It will be Dubai's rail system and the first stage is due to open in 2008, with completion of the project by 2012. It will comprise two lines. One will run up and down the creek, the other will travel along the length of the city from Deira to Jebel Ali Port. All together there will be more than 70km of track and more than 65 stations. BurJuman and Al Ittihad Square stations will link the two lines.

CAR RENTAL

 To rent a car you will need your driver's licence, passport and a credit card. Citizens of most European countries and the US do not require an international driving licence. You must be over 21 to rent a car (25 for larger capacity vehicles). Take out fully comprehensive insurance.

CONCESSIONS

Students/Youths There are very few concessions available in Dubai. Some of the attractions offer a children's rate and some hotels allow children to stay at a reduced rate. Students don't receive any particular discounts and there are no youth hostels.

Senior Citizens There are no special senior discounts. Hotels used to offer discounted accommodation during the broiling summer months, but now rates are beginning to match peak season prices.

DRIVING

 Speed limit on national highways: **120kph**

 Speed limit outside built-up areas: **up to 120kph**

  Speed limit in built-up areas: **60kph**

 Drivers and passengers are legally required to wear seatbelts.

 The police have a zero tolerance policy on drink driving. Never drive under the influence of alcohol.

 Fuel is inexpensive, costing about 6–7Dh per gallon. Filling stations are regularly spaced on most roads.

 Breakdown services cover Dubai: try the AAA (Arabian Automobile Association, www.aaauae.com) or IATC Recovery (International Automobile Touring Club, www.iatcuae.com).

PHOTOGRAPHY

Taking pictures of tourist attractions and other sights is fine, but be careful when it comes to people. It is considered unacceptable to take pictures of Muslim women, and you should ask permission before taking pictures of Muslim men. Photography of government buildings and military installations is forbidden and could land you in serious trouble. Also be wary of taking pictures of sensitive subjects, such as migrant labourers. Memory cards for digital cameras are widely available in shopping malls.

PERSONAL SAFETY

Dubai is one of the safest cities in the world, but take the same precautions you would anywhere else:

- Leave money and valuables in your hotel safe. Carry only what you need and keep it hidden.
- Make copies of important documents and store them separately.
- Take care if driving – Dubai has an appalling road safety record.

Police:
☎ **999**

Ambulance:
☎ **998 and 999**

Fire:
☎ **997**

TELEPHONES

All telephone numbers in Dubai are seven digits, which is all you need to dial within Dubai. But each emirate in the United Arab Emirates has its own code: Abu Dhabi: 02, Ajman: 06, Al Ain: 03, Dubai: 04, Fujairah: 09, Ras Al Khaimah: 07, Sharjah: 06. The international code for Dubai is +971. Mobile phones in Dubai have the code 050. The operator can be dialled on 100 and directory enquiries on 181. Cheap rates for international calls apply 9pm–7am and all day Friday and national holidays.

International Dialling Codes	
From Dubai to:	
UK:	00 44
Germany:	00 49
USA:	00 1
Spain:	00 34

POST

Post within the UAE usually takes 2–3 days, but to Europe, the US and Australia it can take up to 10 days. Buy stamps from post offices and some shops. Hotels will post mail for guests. All incoming mail goes to a post office box and has to be collected.

HEALTH

Insurance
It is essential to take out full health insurance when visiting Dubai. Medical standards in the UAE are high, but the cost of medical treatment is also very high.

Doctors
State healthcare is generally very good. Emergency treatment is provided free of charge, but if you want to see a doctore for a non-emergency consultation you will have to pay 100dh. Many hotels also have their own on-site doctor. Good dentists are also widely available. Ask your hotel to direct you to the nearest one.

Weather
The most important preventative action is to drink a lot water (several litres daily) to reduce the risk of dehydration in the heat. Apply suncream and cover up with a sun hat to minimise the risk of sunstroke.

Drugs
There are pharmacies throughout Dubai, providing many medicines without a prescription. There are no specific diseases to take prevention against. Malarial mosquitoes are present outside cities, but few people take malarial prophylactics.

Safe Water
Tap water is safe to drink. Bottled water is widely available. Local brands are less expensive to buy than international labels.

LANGUAGE

The official language in Dubai is Arabic, but English is widely spoken. People are always happy, and proud, to practise their foreign languages, but even if you only speak a few words of Arabic, you will generally meet with an enthusiastic response. The following is a phonetic transliteration from the Arabic script. Words or letters in brackets indicate the different form that is required when addressing, or speaking as, a woman.

money	niqood	mail	bareed
where is the bank?	ayna al-bank?	cheque	sheak
dirham	dirham	traveller's cheque	sheak siyahi
half a pound	nisf junaih	credit card	bittakat iiteman
small change	fakkah		
post office	maktab al-bareed		

restaurant	mataami	salt and pepper	milh wa filfil
I would like …	oreed an aakul	meat	lahm
alcohol/beer	beerah	breakfast	ifttar
coffee/tea	qahwah/shaay	lunch	ghadaa
mineral water	meeyah maadaniah	dinner	aashaa
milk	haleeb	table	maaida
red wine/white wine	nabeez ahmar/ abyadd	waiter	nadil
		menu	qaaimat at-ttaam
bread	khoubz	bill	fatourah

I'm lost	ana taaih (ana taaiha)	train	qittar
		train station	mahatat al-qitar
where is…?	ayna…?	left/right	yassar/yameen
airport	mattar	straight on	ala tuul
boat	markib	return ticket	tadhkarah zihaab wa rigooa
bus	baass		
street	shaari	car	sayarah
taxi rank	mawqif at-taxi	passport	jawaz as-safar

yes	naam	fine, thank you	bikhayr, shukran
no	laa	God willing	In shaa al-laah
please	min fadlak (min fadlik)	no problem	laa toojad mushkilah
		sorry	aasif (aasifa)
thank you	shukran	excuse me	an idhnak (an idhnik)
you're welcome	afwan	my name is …	ismii…
hello (to Muslims)	as-salamu alaykum	do you speak English?	hal tatakallam al-inglizyah? (hal tatakallamin…)
response	wa-alaykum as-salam		
hello (to Copts)	as-salamu lakum		
welcome	ahlan wa-sahlan	I don't understand	laa afhami
response	ahlan bika (ahlan biki)	I understand	afhami
		I don't speak Arabic	Arabiclaa atakallam al-arabiyyah
goodbye	ma-asalama		
good morning	sabaah al-khayr	help!	tarri!
response	sabaah an-nuur	thief!	an-najdah!
good evening	masaa al-khayr	police	liss
response	masaa an-nuur	go away	ab-eed (ab-eedy)
how are you?	kayfa haalak (kayfa haalik)	leave me alone	atrukni wahdi (atrukeeni wahdi)

REMEMBER

- Departure tax is usually levied by your airline and included in the ticket price.
- It is not essential to confirm your flight before arriving at the airport; many people check in online up to 24 hours in advance.
- Plan to arrive at the airport at least 2 hours before your flight is due to leave, taking into account Dubai's chronic traffic congestion.

Index

TwinPack
Dubai

Written and updated by Robin Barton
Produced by AA Publishing
Editorial management Stephanie Smith
Designer Jacqueline Bailey
Series editor Cathy Hatley

A CIP catalogue record for this book is available from the British Library.

ISBN 978-0-7495-5541-2

Material in this book may have appeared in other AA publications.

Published by AA Publishing, a trading name of Automobile Association Developments Limited, whose registered office is Fanum House, Basing View, Basingstoke, Hampshire RG21 4EA.
Registered number 1878835.

Colour separation by Keenes, Andover
Printed and bound by Everbest Printing Co. Limited, China

ACKNOWLEDGEMENTS
The Automobile Association would like to thank the following photographers, companies and picture libraries for their assistance in the preparation of this book. Abbreviations for the picture credits are as follows: (t) top; (b) bottom; (l) left; (r) right; (AA) AA World Travel Library

1 AA/Clive Sawyer; 5t, 5b AA/Clive Sawyer; 6 AA/Clive Sawyer; 7t, 7b AA/Clive Sawyer; 8 AA/Clive Sawyer; 9 AA/Clive Sawyer; 12t, 12b AA/Clive Sawyer; 13t, 13b AA/Clive Sawyer; 14 Rivi Wickramarachchi/Alamy;15 AA/Clive Sawyer; 17 Robin Barton; 18 AA/Clive Sawyer; 19 AA/Clive Sawyer; 20 AA/Clive Sawyer; 21 AA/Clive Sawyer; 23t, 23b AA/Clive Sawyer; 24t, 24b AA/Clive Sawyer; 25t, 25b AA/Clive Sawyer; 26t Downtown Burj Dubai by Emaar Properties; 26b Photographs provided courtesy of the Government of Dubai Department of Tourism and Commerce Marketing; 27t, 27b AA/Clive Sawyer; 28t, 28b AA/Clive Sawyer; 29t, 29b AA/Clive Sawyer; 30t, 30b AA/Clive Sawyer; 31t, 31b AA/Clive Sawyer; 32t, 32b AA/Clive Sawyer; 33t, 33b AA/Clive Sawyer; 34t, 34b AA/Clive Sawyer; 35t, 35b AA/Clive Sawyer; 36 Robin Barton; 37t, 37b AA/Clive Sawyer; 38t, 38b AA/Clive Sawyer; 39t, 39b AA/Clive Sawyer; 40t, 40b Robin Barton; 41t, 41b AA/Clive Sawyer; 42t, 42b AA/Clive Sawyer; 43 Nakheel; 44t, 44b AA/Clive Sawyer; 45t, 45b AA/Clive Sawyer; 46t, 46b AA/Clive Sawyer; 47 Photographs provided courtesy of the Government of Dubai Department of Tourism and Commerce Marketing; 48 AA/Clive Sawyer; 49t, 49b AA/Clive Sawyer; 50 AA/Clive Sawyer; 51 AA/Clive Sawyer; 52 AA/Clive Sawyer; 54t Ritz-Carlton Hotel; 54b Royal Mirage Hotel, Givenchy Spa; 55 Fairmont Hotel, Willow Stream Spa; 56 AA/Clive Sawyer; 57 AA/Clive Sawyer; 58 AA/Clive Sawyer; 59 AA/Clive Sawyer; 60t, 60b AA/Clive Sawyer; 61t, 61b AA/Clive Sawyer; 84 AA/Clive Sawyer; 85t, 85b AA/Clive Sawyer; 90t, 90cl, 90c AA/Clive Sawyer.
Front and back cover images: AA/Clive Sawyer

Every effort has been made to trace the copyright holders, and we apologise in advance for any accidental errors. We would be happy to apply the corrections in the following edition of this publication.

A03185
Maps in this title produced from map data supplied by Global Mapping, Brackley, UK.
Copyright © Global Mapping/ITMB

TITLES IN THE TWINPACK SERIES
• Algarve • Andalucía • Corfu • Costa Blanca • Costa Brava • Costa del Sol • Crete •
• Croatia • Cyprus • Dubai • Gran Canaria • Lanzarote & Fuerteventura • Madeira •
• Mallorca • Malta & Gozo • Menorca • Provence & the Côte d'Azur • Tenerife •

Dear **TwinPack** Traveller

Your comments, opinions and recommendations are very important to us. So please help us to improve our travel guides by taking a few minutes to complete this simple questionnaire.

You do not need a stamp (unless posted outside the UK). If you do not want to cut this page from your guide, then photocopy it or write your answers on a plain sheet of paper.

Send to: **The Editor, AA TwinPack Travel Guides, FREEPOST SCE 4598, Basingstoke RG21 4GY.**

Your recommendations...

We always encourage readers' recommendations for restaurants, nightlife or shopping – if your recommendation is used in the next edition of the guide, we will send you a *FREE* **AA TwinPack Guide** of your choice. Please state below the establishment name, location and your reasons for recommending it.

_____

_____

_____

_____

Please send me **AA TwinPack**

Algarve ☐   Andalucía ☐   Corfu ☐   Costa Blanca ☐
Costa Brava ☐   Costa del Sol ☐   Crete ☐   Croatia ☐
Cyprus ☐   Dubai ☐   Gran Canaria ☐   Lanzarote & Fuerteventura ☐
Madeira ☐   Mallorca ☐   Malta & Gozo ☐   Menorca ☐
Provence & the Côte d'Azur ☐   Tenerife ☐
(please tick as appropriate)

About this guide...

Which title did you buy?
AA *TwinPack* _____
Where did you buy it? _____
When? m m / y y

Why did you choose an AA *TwinPack* Guide? _____

_____

_____

_____

Did this guide meet your expectations?
Exceeded ☐   Met all ☐   Met most ☐   Fell below ☐
Please give your reasons _____

_____

_____

continued on next page...

Were there any aspects of this guide that you particularly liked? _____

_____

_____

Is there anything we could have done better? _____

_____

_____

About you…

Name *(Mr/Mrs/Ms)* _____

Address _____

_____

_____ Postcode _____

Daytime tel no _____

Please only give us your mobile phone number if you wish to hear from us about other products and services from the AA and partners by text or mms.

Which age group are you in?

Under 25 ☐ 25–34 ☐ 35–44 ☐ 45–54 ☐ 55–64 ☐ 65+ ☐

How many trips do you make a year?

None ☐ One ☐ Two ☐ Three or more ☐

Are you an AA member? Yes ☐ No ☐

About your trip…

When did you book? m m / y y   When did you travel? m m / y y

How long did you stay? _____

Was it for business or leisure? _____

Did you buy any other travel guides for your trip?

If yes, which ones? _____

Thank you for taking the time to complete this questionnaire. Please send it to us as soon as possible, and remember, you do not need a stamp *(unless posted outside the UK)*.

Happy Holidays!